The Fathers Nobody Warned

Intrusive Thoughts, Harm OCD, and the First Two Years of Being a Dad

Mason R. Ellery

This book is provided for general informational and educational purposes. It does not diagnose any person and does not provide individualized medical, psychological, psychiatric, legal, or emergency advice. It is not a substitute for evaluation or treatment by a qualified professional.

No outcome is guaranteed. Mental-health symptoms, family circumstances, and treatment needs differ. Readers remain responsible for decisions about care, safety, and professional support.

If you have intent or planning to harm yourself or another person, a wish to act, loss of contact with reality, severe impairment, or any reason you are unsure that you or a child can be kept safe, seek urgent in-person help through appropriate local services. Medication decisions belong with a qualified prescriber.

Names and scenarios in this book are composites created for illustration. They are not accounts of identifiable individuals and are not intended to portray or misrepresent any person or organization.

ISBN: 978-1-911838-74-6

Table of Contents

Preface

Research on intrusive thoughts around the arrival of a child has a long imbalance. Maternal experiences have received most of the attention, while fathers appear far less often in the evidence base and in routine perinatal mental-health pathways. Yet mixed-parent studies and clinical case reports show that new fathers can experience unwanted infant-related intrusions, compulsive responses, and, in some cases, obsessive-compulsive disorder. The gap is not proof that fathers experience a unique disorder. It is a reason to be precise about what is known, what remains uncertain, and what a father can do when fear begins changing how he parents.

An intrusive thought is an unwanted thought, image, urge, or doubt that enters awareness without being deliberately chosen. Harm OCD refers to an OCD presentation in which obsessions center on causing or being responsible for harm and are followed by compulsions intended to reduce doubt or distress. In early fatherhood, those compulsions may be visible, such as avoiding bath time or refusing solo care, or largely mental, such as reviewing a nappy change, checking a body sensation, or asking a partner for reassurance. The content of a thought is not enough to diagnose OCD or settle a safety question. Intent, planning, behavior, reality testing, other symptoms, and the full clinical pattern matter.

This book fills a practical gap between general OCD material and fatherhood advice that never mentions obsessional fear. Its central tool is the Stay-In Ladder, a way to identify a valued parenting task, break re-entry into observable steps, and reduce the compulsive responses attached to those steps. The method is built around participation rather than emotional certainty. It is intended to help a father see when reasonable childcare safety has been replaced by a private demand for absolute proof.

The primary reader is a new father who has begun withdrawing from ordinary care because a frightening thought feels like evidence about his character or risk. Partners may also use the book to understand reassurance, avoidance, and family accommodation. Clinicians may find the father-specific examples useful as conversation starters, but this is not a clinical manual.

This book provides education, language, and structured reflection. It does not diagnose you, determine whether a particular thought is safe, prescribe treatment, or replace individualized medical or mental-health care. If you have intent or planning to harm, a wish to act, loss of contact with reality, severe impairment, or any reason you are unsure someone can be kept safe, seek urgent in-person help. When the pattern is obsessional, a qualified professional can assess it and discuss evidence-based care, including cognitive behavioral therapy with exposure and response prevention where appropriate.

The purpose of these pages is to help you stop letting obsessional doubt quietly decide how much fatherhood you are allowed to do.

Introduction: The Thought That Changed the Room

The room did not look dangerous. A plastic baby bath sat inside the larger tub. A hooded towel hung over the radiator. A bottle of wash was open on the floor because somebody had forgotten to put the cap back on. Aaron's daughter kicked once, splashing his T-shirt, and his wife laughed from the doorway.

Then Aaron had a thought he did not invite.

It was brief. It was about harm. He felt sick before he had even finished registering it. His hands went still. A few seconds later he told his wife that his back was hurting and asked her to take over.

Nothing dramatic happened that night. He did not tell anyone what had gone through his mind. He did not search for a diagnosis. He did not decide, in a single clear moment, that he would never bathe his daughter again. He simply found a reason not to do it the next evening. Two nights after that, he washed the bottles instead. By the end of the week he had become very efficient at setting out pajamas, refilling the nappy station, and tidying the kitchen while somebody else handled the bath.

From the outside, he looked helpful. From the inside, a rule was forming: a good father does not put himself in a situation where that thought could matter.

That rule is where this book begins.

Intrusive thoughts are unwanted thoughts, images, urges, or doubts that arrive in awareness without being chosen. New parenthood supplies the mind with a vast amount of threat material because a baby is small, dependent, unpredictable, and important. A prospective study of 85 new mothers and fathers found that the majority reported intrusive infant-related thoughts and neutralizing behavior, although the experiences described were generally less severe than those seen in obsessive-compulsive disorder (OCD) (Abramowitz et al., 2006). A small 2001 case series also described four men whose OCD began around a spouse's pregnancy or delivery, showing that postpartum-onset obsessional problems are not limited to mothers (Abramowitz et al., 2001).

Those findings establish possibility, not a precise father-specific prevalence rate. The paternal evidence base is still thin. A UK Health Research Authority study summary written specifically about intrusive harm thoughts in new fathers notes that research had focused mainly on mothers and that very few empirical studies had investigated the experience in fathers (Health Research Authority, 2020). That gap matters because a father searching for an explanation often finds either general OCD information or perinatal material written around mothers.

The International OCD Foundation now describes perinatal OCD as something that can affect parents of any gender and lists avoidance among possible compulsions, including not holding a baby, not bathing the baby, and not spending time alone with the baby (International OCD Foundation, n.d.). That is a clinically recognizable pattern. It is also easy to misread in a family. A partner sees a father refusing another nappy change. The father experiences himself as preventing catastrophe. Both may be exhausted. Neither may have a name for the mechanism between them.

This book gives that mechanism a name without pretending a book can diagnose you.

The Question Is Not Only What You Thought

Harm OCD is a common informal label for OCD in which obsessions center on causing harm or failing to prevent it. The content can be violent, accidental, sexual, contamination-related, moral, religious, or organized around losing control. The theme matters because it shapes what a person avoids. The clinical process matters more because two people can have a similar unwanted thought and respond to it very differently.

One person notices a disturbing mental event, dislikes it, and gets pulled back into the next task. Another person treats the event as evidence. He checks how he felt. He tests his memory. He searches online. He asks his partner whether she thinks he is a good father. He avoids the object that was present when the thought appeared. He stops being alone with the baby. The thought becomes the opening move in a repeated sequence.

In OCD language, obsessions are intrusive experiences that generate distress, and compulsions are behaviors or mental acts performed to reduce that distress, prevent a feared outcome, or gain certainty. Compulsions can be obvious, such as checking a lock. They can also be private: replaying a memory, reviewing whether you felt the "wrong" sensation, silently arguing with a thought, comparing yourself with a news story, or asking the same moral question in slightly different words.

The loop is important because reassurance can turn into part of the problem. So can avoidance. If every frightening thought leads to retreat, the mind never gets a chance to learn that ordinary parenting can continue without a certificate of total certainty.

That does not mean every avoided situation should be entered, and it does not mean every disturbing thought is OCD. A responsible book about this subject has to hold two facts at once. First, unwanted intrusive thoughts and obsessional doubt are well described in OCD and early parenthood. Second, thought content alone cannot establish whether somebody is safe, has OCD, is depressed, is psychotic, is dealing with anger, or needs another form of care.

Clinicians consider the whole presentation. Desire, intent, planning, behavior, insight, reality testing, mood symptoms, substance use, sleep, and other factors can change what the next step should be. If you want to act on a harmful thought, have formed a plan, feel unable to control your behavior, are hearing commands, are experiencing beliefs or perceptions that other people do not share, or cannot keep yourself or a child safe, this book is not the right tool for that moment. Seek urgent in-person assessment.

The point of that boundary is not to frighten you. It is to keep a self-help book in its proper role.

Why Fatherhood Can Make the Question Feel Unbearable

A baby changes the moral weight of uncertainty. Before becoming a father, you may have been able to accept that accidents happen, that people get strange thoughts, and that nobody controls every risk. Once a small person depends on you, the demand can change. Your mind may insist that an acceptable father should know, beyond doubt, that he will never make a dangerous mistake and never discover something terrible about himself.

No human being can meet that standard.

OCD can exploit the gap between ordinary responsibility and impossible responsibility. It asks for more checking, more certainty, more avoidance, more analysis. The father often cooperates because the subject is his child. What could be more responsible than being careful?

Carefulness becomes costly when the rule has no finish line.

You check the baby monitor once because the screen froze. That is ordinary problem solving. You check it thirty times because the last twenty-nine checks did not produce permanent certainty. The external action looks similar; the function is different. You ask your partner to handle a bath because you are ill. That is division of labor. You give up baths for months because the absence of a frightening thought has become a condition for participation. Again, the function is different.

This book will keep returning to function. What is this behavior trying to accomplish? What certainty is it trying to manufacture? What part of fatherhood is shrinking while you wait for the certainty to arrive?

The Stay-In Ladder

The central tool in the book is the Stay-In Ladder. It is a way of thinking about re-entry into ordinary, lawful, developmentally appropriate parenting tasks that fear has pushed you away from. A rung is not a stunt. It is not deliberate contact with genuine danger. It is not permission to ignore normal childcare safety. It is a practical question: what ordinary thing would you be doing if the demand for impossible certainty were not setting the rules?

For Aaron, the answer was not "prove I am safe." It was "be present for bath time."

The Stay-In Ladder begins with a parenting value, identifies an avoided task, and then looks for the compulsions attached to that task. A first rung might involve remaining in the room instead of escaping it, completing a normal care step instead of handing it over, or reducing one reassurance request. In formal OCD treatment, exposure and response prevention (ERP) is a form of cognitive behavioral therapy that pairs planned contact with feared cues or situations with prevention of the compulsive response. NICE recommends CBT including ERP among treatment options for adults with OCD, with treatment intensity based on impairment and preference (National Institute for Health and Care Excellence, 2005).

This book borrows the logic of graded re-entry and response prevention for explanation. It does not attempt to replace individualized ERP. If symptoms are severe, if risk is unclear, if you have significant depression or other mental-health symptoms, or if an exercise involving your child feels clinically complicated, the responsible move is to work with a qualified professional who understands OCD.

What This Book Will Not Ask You to Do

It will not ask you to convince yourself that every thought is harmless. That would turn the book into a reassurance object.

It will not ask you to confess every detail of every thought to your partner. Confession can itself become a compulsion.

It will not tell you that anger is "how OCD looks in men." A small qualitative study of fathers with postpartum depression reported anger and frustration in some participants, but that is not evidence for a male-specific harm-OCD presentation (Pedersen et al., 2021). Anger, depression, sleep loss, trauma symptoms, substance use, OCD, and relationship conflict can overlap, but they are not interchangeable.

It will not pretend that the formal perinatal period necessarily lasts for the entire two years covered by this book. Research definitions often end at twelve months postpartum. The two-year span here is a practical parenting scope. It follows the problem from newborn care into crawling, walking, solid food, playgrounds, tantrums, and the other changes that can give the same doubt new material.

Most of all, it will not ask you to become certain before you become involved.

The better question is smaller and harder: when uncertainty is present, what does responsible fathering ask you to do next?

PART I: WHAT THE THOUGHT MEANS

From shocking content to a workable understanding of the loop.

Chapter 1: The Bath-Time Thought

Aaron's new rule lasted twelve days before his wife noticed it.

He still came upstairs at seven. He still carried the clean nappy and the pajamas. He filled the tub, checked the water, and laid the towel on the floor. Then, at the point where somebody had to lift their daughter into the bath, Aaron found another job.

On the first night, he answered a work message. On the second, he said he would clear dinner. By the sixth, he no longer needed an excuse because the new arrangement had become routine. His wife did the bath. Aaron handled everything around it.

The thought itself had lasted perhaps a second. What occupied the next twelve days was his attempt to decide what the second meant.

Did it mean he had wanted it? Did the fact that it had appeared while his baby was vulnerable make it worse? Would a safe father even be capable of picturing such a thing? He inspected his memory for disgust. Then he inspected the disgust. Was it immediate enough? Strong enough? Was he manufacturing it now because he knew what he was supposed to feel?

By day twelve, the original thought was less vivid than the investigation.

That distinction matters. An intrusive thought can be brief. The response to it can become a full-time job.

A Mental Event and the Story Built Around It

An intrusive thought is an unwanted thought, image, impulse, urge, or doubt that arrives without deliberate choice. The word intrusive describes how the event shows up, not what it secretly proves. A mental event can be disturbing precisely because it conflicts with what matters to you.

Research with new parents gives us a useful starting point, though not a father-only estimate. In the prospective study by Abramowitz and colleagues, most of the 85 new mothers and fathers reported infant-related intrusive thoughts and some form of neutralizing behavior. Their experiences were generally less severe than clinical OCD (Abramowitz et al., 2006). Earlier work also described obsessional problems in new fathers, including a four-case report in which male OCD onset coincided with a partner's pregnancy or delivery (Abramowitz et al., 2001).

Those studies do not tell us that every new father with a disturbing thought has OCD. They tell us something more modest and useful: fatherhood does not place men outside the territory of intrusive infant-related thoughts and obsessional responses.

The difference between a passing intrusion and an obsessional problem is not a simple content test. People without OCD can have bizarre, violent, sexual, or morally offensive thoughts. People with OCD can have ordinary-sounding doubts that become consuming. The diagnostic question belongs to a clinician and depends on the wider pattern: repetition, distress, time, impairment, compulsions, avoidance, and the way the person relates to the experience.

Aaron made the content the entire case. "A person who had this thought during a bath must be dangerous." Once he accepted that premise, every later behavior made sense. Of course he should hand over bath time. Of course he should check his memory. Of course he should watch his own body and emotions. The hidden premise never received the same scrutiny as the checking.

That is one reason OCD can feel so morally persuasive. The conclusion arrives first. The investigation is hired to support it.

Four Separate Things

When a thought frightens you, it helps to separate four elements that anxiety tends to fuse together.

First is the content: what appeared in your mind.

Second is the meaning: what you decided the appearance said about you, the future, or your level of responsibility.

Third is the feeling: fear, disgust, shame, guilt, numbness, uncertainty, or some mixture.

Fourth is the response: what you did next, including what you did only in your head.

Take a father standing near a staircase with his baby. An unwanted image appears of the baby falling. The content is the image. The meaning may be, "I pictured it because part of me could do it." The feeling is panic and disgust. The response may be to hand the baby to his partner, grip the banister in a special way, replay where his hands were, and avoid carrying the child upstairs again.

The image matters because it is upsetting. The long-term pattern is built from the meaning and response.

This four-part separation is not a trick for proving safety. Do not turn it into a courtroom where you repeatedly classify each thought until you feel clean. Use it once to make the process visible. Then ask the more useful question: what response is teaching my brain that this thought requires emergency treatment?

Unwanted Does Not Mean "Ignore Everything"

People sometimes hear the phrase unwanted thought and use it as a shortcut: "If I hate the thought, then I am definitely safe." A self-help book should not hand out that certificate.

The unwanted, ego-dystonic quality of obsessions is clinically important. In maternal postpartum literature, insight and distress about intrusive harm obsessions are part of the differential picture separating OCD from psychotic states involving delusions or hallucinations (Hudak & Wisner, 2012). But a clinician does not assess risk from one adjective. They consider intent, desire, planning, behavior, reality testing, mood, substance use, and other information.

For a reader, the practical rule is plain. If you are frightened by a thought and responding with checking, avoidance, or reassurance, that is information worth taking to an OCD-informed professional. If you want to act, have a plan, are losing touch with reality, are hearing commands, or cannot keep yourself or your child safe, seek urgent in-person assessment.

That boundary lets us discuss OCD without making the opposite mistake of treating every disturbing mental event as a danger signal.

The Theme Can Change Without the Process Changing

A new father's obsessions do not have to look like a crime-thriller version of harm. They can be organized around accident, contamination, illness, sexuality, morality, religion, or the fear of losing control.

One father refuses to stand on a balcony with his baby because of a sudden image of dropping him. Another sterilizes feeding equipment far beyond ordinary guidance because any uncertainty about contamination feels unacceptable. Another checks the baby's breathing over and over, not because anything has changed, but because the last check stopped working emotionally. Another avoids nappy changes because a taboo sexual thought made him afraid of his own attention and bodily sensations.

The themes are different. The bargain is similar: "I will do something extra, or stop doing something ordinary, until I feel certain."

Certainty is the product that never arrives.

That is why changing themes can be so confusing. A father may believe he recovered from one fear because bath time no longer bothers him, only to find himself trapped in car-seat checking. He may think the new content proves the old explanation was wrong. In fact, the process may have found new material.

The aim is not to win against every possible thought. It is to change what happens after the thought knocks.

An Action You Can Take Without Arguing With the Thought

Think of one recent episode, preferably not your most distressing one. Write four short lines.

Content: What showed up?

Meaning: What did I decide it meant?

Feeling: What did I notice emotionally or physically?

Response: What did I do to reduce doubt or prevent the feared outcome?

Then add a fifth line: Cost.

Cost means what the response took from you. Minutes lost to checking. A care task handed to your partner. A room you stopped entering. Sleep used for research. A conversation turned into interrogation. A nappy change you wanted to be able to do but did not.

The Cost line keeps this exercise from becoming another analysis ritual. You are not trying to prove why the thought came. You are looking at what your current response is purchasing and what it is charging you.

Aaron's page looked like this in substance. Content: an unwanted harm image during the bath. Meaning: a safe father would not have pictured it. Feeling: shock, nausea, shame, doubt. Response: leave bath time, check memory, watch emotions, search for certainty.

Cost: twelve nights outside a part of fatherhood he had expected to share.

That last line changed the conversation.

The Mind Loves Retroactive Evidence

After a frightening thought, memory often becomes a crime scene. You rewind. You examine the second before the thought. You ask whether you were angry. You inspect the exact position of your hands. You try to recover what you "really" felt.

This can feel like responsible fact-finding, especially when the subject is your child. Yet repeated mental review is not a neutral act. Each review teaches the mind that the memory has unresolved legal status.

Suppose you remember being irritated because your baby would not settle. Hours later an intrusive image appears. The OCD-style interpretation connects them: "I was angry, then I had the image, so the image must reveal what the anger could make me do." Now irritation itself becomes suspicious. The next time you feel frustrated, you monitor it. The monitoring increases self-consciousness. A normal flash of impatience starts to feel like a warning siren.

That does not mean anger is irrelevant. How you behave when angry matters. If you are shouting, breaking things, frightening people, or fear losing control, treat that as a real behavior and safety issue deserving direct help. But do not use a normal human emotion as a laboratory test for the truth of an obsession.

A father can be exhausted, annoyed, loving, frightened, and responsible in the same afternoon. Fatherhood does not make emotional purity possible.

Why Reassurance Feels Like an Answer

Aaron eventually told his wife a softened version of what had happened. He said, "I had a weird thought in the bath and now I keep worrying it means something."

She answered immediately: "Of course it doesn't. You would never hurt her."

For twenty minutes, Aaron felt lighter.

Then a new question appeared. Had he explained the thought accurately enough? If she knew the exact wording, would she still say the same thing? Was her reassurance valid if she was biased because she loved him?

He returned to the conversation.

This is the reassurance loop. The answer can be sincere, kind, and completely accurate from the partner's point of view. The problem is the job Aaron gives it: end uncertainty permanently.

No human sentence can do that.

A reassurance loop often escalates by demanding finer detail. "But what if I felt calm for half a second?" "What if I didn't pull away immediately?" "What if the fact I need reassurance is evidence?" Each answer reduces distress briefly and teaches the brain to ask another question.

Later chapters will deal with partner reassurance directly. For now, notice the design flaw. If certainty is the required outcome, no answer is durable enough.

The First Principle of Staying In

A father who has stepped back often thinks the first task is to feel normal again. He waits for the thought to stop appearing, for disgust to feel exactly right, for confidence to return.

That order can keep him waiting.

The first principle of the Stay-In Ladder is that participation does not have to wait for a perfect internal state. The question is whether there is an ordinary, appropriate parenting action that can be chosen without performing the extra behavior demanded by fear.

For Aaron, the first change was small. He did not take over the entire bath alone. He stayed in the room. He handed over the washcloth. He noticed the urge to ask, "You know I would never...?" and did not ask it.

His anxiety rose. It also changed on its own timetable.

More important, the evening ended with a completed act of care rather than another successful escape.

That is not a dramatic recovery story. It is better than one. It is a repeatable unit of behavior.

The Question Under the Question

There is usually a second question underneath the one a frightened father says out loud.

The spoken question may be, "Why did I think that?" The hidden question is often, "Can I obtain a kind of certainty about myself that no human being can actually obtain?"

Tomas noticed this after a different trigger. He had been carrying his sleeping son from the car when a sudden unwanted doubt appeared about losing control. He set the carrier down safely, then spent the next hour trying to decide whether the doubt had felt like a thought or an urge. He searched definitions. He compared descriptions from strangers online. He asked himself whether he had felt a movement in his arm.

None of the research changed the external event. His son had been carried from the car. What changed was Tomas's standard of proof. By midnight, ordinary uncertainty was no longer acceptable. He wanted an internal recording that could show every sensation, intention, and microsecond of the experience.

That recording does not exist.

This is where a useful observation can become a compulsion. It is reasonable to notice patterns and tell a clinician what happens. It is not reasonable to expect memory to deliver a perfect forensic record of mental life. The more a person tries to recover certainty from memory, the more important every gap can seem.

If you recognize that process, try a different sentence: "I notice that my mind is asking for evidence I cannot collect." Do not use the sentence to force relief. Use it to identify the task you are being invited to refuse.

Then return to something concrete. Put the bottle in the sterilizer. Fold the sleep suit. Read the board book. Ask your partner how their day was without turning the answer into a discussion of your thought. The return is not avoidance of the problem. It is refusal to spend another hour serving a question with no stopping rule.

That distinction will matter throughout the book. We are not trying to make you care less about safety. We are trying to separate ordinary responsibility from an endless internal trial.

Principles to Remember

An intrusive thought is a mental event. The obsessional problem grows from the meaning attached to it and the responses used to obtain certainty.

Do not use the content alone to diagnose yourself or to perform your own risk assessment. Unwanted, distressing thoughts can occur in OCD and in people without OCD. If there is desire, intent, planning, loss of reality testing, command experiences, or inability to keep a child safe, urgent in-person help is the appropriate next step.

If the pattern looks like fear followed by avoidance, checking, reassurance, or mental review, notice the cost. The first useful move may not be explaining the thought. It may be identifying the part of fatherhood your response is making smaller.

The thought may have opened the door. The repeated response is what keeps the room occupied.

Chapter 2: The Dad Nobody Screens

Ben sat through six appointments in which everybody asked some version of the same sensible questions. How was the pregnancy going? Was his partner sleeping? Did they have support at home? Had they chosen a pediatrician? Did they know the signs that meant the baby needed medical attention?

Ben learned a lot. He learned how to support a head during a bath and how to fasten a car-seat harness. He learned that newborns make noises in their sleep that sound alarming. He learned which number to call if feeding became a problem.

Nobody asked what had started happening in his own mind.

By the third week after the birth, Ben had a repeated unwanted image whenever he stood at the top of the stairs with his daughter. By week five, he had stopped carrying her downstairs. He told his partner that his knee felt unstable. She believed him because he had complained about that knee before.

He did not feel entitled to make the problem about himself. His partner was recovering from birth. The baby needed everything. Ben's job, as he understood it, was to make life easier. Admitting that his own mind had become a problem felt like stealing attention from the people who had a stronger claim on it.

That belief is larger than OCD. It belongs to the culture of fatherhood, the organization of perinatal care, and the ways men often understand help-seeking. It is also one reason father-specific intrusive thoughts can remain invisible.

The Research Gap Is Real

The scientific literature on perinatal OCD has historically concentrated on mothers. That is not surprising. Pregnancy, childbirth, postpartum physiology, and maternal mental health have direct clinical importance, and maternal populations have been studied far more extensively.

The danger comes when absence of father-specific data gets mistaken for absence of the phenomenon.

A 2001 report described four men whose OCD began around a spouse's pregnancy or delivery. The authors noted that research on postpartum-onset OCD had focused exclusively on women and that the men's obsessions and compulsions resembled patterns reported in female samples (Abramowitz et al., 2001). A later prospective study followed 85 new mothers and fathers through childbirth and the postpartum period. Most reported intrusive infant-related thoughts and neutralizing behaviors, usually at a lower level than clinical OCD (Abramowitz et al., 2006).

Those are meaningful findings, but they are not a modern, nationally representative prevalence study of paternal harm OCD.

The UK Health Research Authority registered a study titled Intrusive Thoughts of Harm in New Fathers and summarized the state of the field plainly: maternal intrusive thoughts had received most of the research attention, evidence suggested similar experiences may occur in fathers, and very few empirical studies had examined new fathers directly (Health Research Authority, 2020).

That sentence should change how we talk about the topic. We can say fathers can experience obsessional problems around a baby's arrival. We can say mixed-parent research has found intrusive infant-related thoughts and neutralizing. We can say the father-specific evidence base is limited.

We should not invent a precise percentage to make the book sound more authoritative.

The International OCD Foundation currently states that perinatal OCD can affect fathers, same-sex partners, adoptive parents, and other non-birthing parents. Its educational page gives an estimate of about 2 to 3 percent of all parents (International OCD Foundation, n.d.). That figure should not be read as a father-specific prevalence estimate. Because the paternal evidence remains limited and the page does not report a separate paternal denominator, this book does not convert that figure into "2 to 3 percent of fathers." Father-specific prevalence remains uncertain.

That uncertainty is not a weakness. It is information.

The Problem of Being the Secondary Patient

Perinatal systems are built around pregnancy, birth, infant health, and the birthing parent's recovery. Much of that structure is medically necessary. A father may nevertheless absorb a social message from it: you are here as support, not as someone whose own mental health belongs in the room.

Research on paternal perinatal depression makes that broader context visible. An updated meta-analysis of 74 studies involving 41,480 participants estimated paternal depression during pregnancy and the first year postpartum at 8.4 percent, while also finding substantial variation across methods and settings (Cameron et al., 2016). An earlier meta-analysis produced a higher pooled estimate and found an association between paternal and maternal depression (Paulson & Bazemore, 2010). These are depression findings, not OCD findings, but they show that fathers are not psychologically irrelevant during the transition to parenthood.

More recent work on help-seeking describes obstacles that will sound familiar to many men: stigma, masculine expectations, limited awareness, uncertainty about where to go, fear of not being taken seriously, and services that are experienced as oriented primarily toward mothers (Reay et al., 2024).

Ben's reasoning fit that pattern. He did not think, "Men should never ask for help." He thought, "This is not the moment for me to be the problem."

That sentence is more difficult to challenge because it contains generosity. He wanted to protect his partner from another burden. He wanted to be useful.

The cost was that he became less useful in exactly the area he was trying to protect.

When Secrecy Looks Like Competence

A father can hide distress remarkably well when he has tasks to perform.

He can order formula, book appointments, research sleep sacks, wash bottles, take out bins, and answer work messages. Those activities create visible evidence of competence. The invisible part can grow at the same time.

One father refuses to hold the baby near an open window but becomes obsessive about assembling furniture correctly. Another avoids nappy changes while volunteering for every grocery run. Another takes every late work call because work is the one place where he does not have to inspect his thoughts around the baby.

The family may experience him as distant. He experiences himself as compensating.

This is why the phrase disengaged father can miss the mechanism. Sometimes a father is disengaged because he does not want to participate. Sometimes he is exhausted, depressed, resentful, frightened, or overwhelmed. Sometimes avoidance is serving an obsessional rule. The outward behavior does not settle the internal cause.

A useful book does not excuse the behavior because fear is underneath it. A partner still has to do the bath. A baby still needs care. The practical goal is to understand the mechanism well enough to change the behavior.

Ben's knee story protected him from disclosure, but it also transferred every staircase trip to his partner. The explanation mattered. So did the workload.

The Social Risk of Saying the Thought Out Loud

Harm OCD has a disclosure problem in any population. A person may fear that violent or taboo content will be mistaken for desire. For a father speaking about his child, that fear can feel amplified by the social responsibility attached to child safety.

It would be dishonest to tell you that every person will respond perfectly. Friends may not understand OCD. Partners may be frightened by unfamiliar language. Clinicians vary in experience. A poorly informed listener can focus on content without asking how the thought is experienced or what follows it.

That is a reason to improve disclosure, not a reason to keep the problem secret indefinitely.

A competent assessment does not stop at "What thought did you have?" It asks what the thought means to you, whether it is wanted or unwanted, whether there is intent or planning, what behaviors follow, what your insight is like, how functioning has changed, and whether other symptoms are present.

You do not need to deliver a lecture on OCD at the appointment. You can begin with a functional description:

"I am having repeated unwanted thoughts about harm involving my baby. They frighten me, and I have started avoiding carrying her on the stairs and checking my reactions. I need an assessment from someone who understands OCD and can also assess safety properly."

That sentence does four useful things. It names the content category without graphic detail. It names that the thoughts are unwanted. It describes the behavior. It asks for assessment rather than asking the clinician to agree with a self-diagnosis.

If the first professional does not understand, that is discouraging. It is not a verdict on the problem.

What "Paternal" Does and Does Not Mean Here

This book uses paternal in a practical sense: it is about the experience of being a father or father-role parent during early parenthood. The scientific literature does not always use the word in the same way. Studies may define fathers biologically, by cohabitation, by sex or gender, or by relationship to a birthing parent. Some perinatal research includes non-birthing partners more broadly. Some does not.

That variation matters when we make claims.

The father-specific examples in this book are written to reach men who identify as dads, including men who became fathers through birth, adoption, or surrogacy. But not every research finding can automatically be generalized across all those paths. Where the evidence concerns biological fathers around a partner's pregnancy, it will be described that way. Where it concerns mothers, it will be identified as maternal evidence. Where the sample mixes mothers and fathers, we will not pretend the father subgroup was studied separately if it was not.

Good science sometimes sounds less satisfying because it contains fewer grand statements. For a topic built around doubt, that restraint is useful.

A Note on the Two-Year Window

Perinatal is not a universal synonym for the first two years. Research definitions vary, and many paternal depression studies and clinical services use pregnancy through twelve months postpartum. The title of this book extends further for a practical reason, not because it is redefining a diagnostic period.

The second year changes the stage on which the same processes can play out.

A newborn lies where you put him. A toddler climbs. A newborn's care is repetitive. A toddler invents new ways to test your tolerance for uncertainty. Kitchens, playgrounds, stairs, bath water, rough play, and sudden movement can all become material for obsessional doubt.

If a father learns only, "My bath-time fear is the problem," he may be blindsided when the bath becomes easy and the playground becomes hard.

If he learns, "My mind is demanding certainty, and I am responding with avoidance and checking," he has something more portable.

That is why the book follows the first two years.

The Appointment Ben Finally Made

Ben did not begin by telling his partner everything. He began with one sentence at breakfast: "My knee is not why I am avoiding the stairs."

His partner stopped pouring cereal.

He told her he was having unwanted harm images and that he had started arranging the day around them. He did not ask her whether she thought he was dangerous. That question was already waiting in his mouth. Instead he said, "I want to talk to somebody who understands OCD."

The conversation was not instantly soothing. His partner had questions. Ben had the urge to answer each question with enough detail to force certainty for both of them. They agreed on something more practical. He would contact his primary-care doctor and look for an OCD specialist. They would discuss childcare workload separately from the content of every intrusive thought.

The next day he made the appointment.

The important part of this story is not that Ben found the perfect service. He did not. His first referral was to a general therapist who had limited OCD experience. He had to ask again.

The important part is that he stopped using the service gap as evidence that the problem did not belong in care.

Your One-Paragraph Brief

Before you contact a professional, write a short brief for yourself. Keep it functional.

Start with when the problem began.

Name the kind of thoughts or doubts in non-graphic language.

State what you do in response: avoid, check, ask for reassurance, review memories, confess, research, monitor sensations, or something else.

State what has changed in your life: time lost, childcare avoided, sleep affected, work used as escape, relationship strain.

Then write what you want from the appointment: assessment for OCD and other relevant mental-health concerns, a safety assessment if needed, and information about evidence-based treatment.

Do not polish the paragraph until it feels morally perfect. Its job is not to prove anything about your character. Its job is to help another person see the pattern.

If the Word OCD Feels Too Big

Some fathers resist the term because it sounds like a claim they have not earned. That is sensible. You do not need to decide the diagnosis before asking for help.

Describe the pattern first. "I get unwanted thoughts. I am avoiding care. I keep checking what the thoughts mean. This is interfering with fatherhood." A professional can work from that information.

The label is useful when it improves treatment selection and understanding. It becomes unhelpful when you use it as another certainty test: "Do I definitely have OCD, and if I do, does that definitely prove what the thought means?" Diagnosis is not a moral certificate. It is a clinical formulation based on a wider assessment.

You are allowed to arrive at an appointment with a question rather than an answer.

Principles to Remember

The father-specific evidence base for perinatal OCD is smaller than the maternal literature. That justifies caution, not silence.

We have evidence that new fathers can experience intrusive infant-related thoughts and obsessional problems. We also have broader paternal mental-health evidence showing that help-seeking can be limited by stigma, role expectations, lack of awareness, and services that fathers may experience as mother-centered.

Do not turn the absence of a perfect father-specific pathway into a reason to wait until your family has reorganized itself around avoidance.

Your problem is allowed to belong in the room even when somebody else in the room also needs care.

Chapter 3: The Alarm Is Not a Verdict

Darius was halfway down the stairs when his mind produced a sentence so fast that it felt less like language than an alarm.

What if you let go?

He stopped on the landing. His son was warm against his chest, one cheek pressed into Darius's shirt. Nothing in Darius wanted to let go. That should have ended the matter.

It did not.

The question changed shape before he reached the ground floor. What if the reason the thought frightened him was that it had revealed a possibility he needed to guard against? What if responsible fathers did not have to guard against themselves? What if the very fact that he was now analyzing it meant he knew something was wrong?

By lunch, Darius was not investigating a staircase. He was investigating his character.

That shift from "I had a thought" to "the thought is evidence" is one of the most important cognitive moves in obsessional problems. It can happen so quickly that the interpretation feels fused to the original event.

The alarm rings. Then the mind mistakes the volume for a verdict.

Thought-Action Fusion

Psychologists use the term thought-action fusion for a family of beliefs in which thoughts and actions are given a relationship they do not logically have. One form is moral: thinking about an unacceptable act feels morally similar to performing it. Another form is probabilistic: having a thought feels as though it makes the event more likely. Thought-action fusion has been studied in relation to obsessional problems, although it is not unique to OCD (Shafran & Rachman, 2004).

The concept is useful because it explains why a father can react to a mental event as if it were behavior.

Darius did not merely dislike the staircase thought. He treated its appearance as a data point about what he might do. Once that happened, his next move was obvious: collect more data.

He checked his emotional reaction. He reviewed whether his arms had moved. He tried to remember whether the thought had been an image, an urge, or a sentence. He asked whether he had felt an instant of curiosity before fear. The more he inspected, the more distinctions he discovered. Each distinction opened another question.

The goal was safety. The method was an unlimited audit.

One problem with this audit is that mental life is noisy. A person can have a sensation without knowing exactly why. An image can appear without a story attached to it. A thought can arrive while you are angry, bored, affectionate, hungry, or thinking about something else. If every mental event must be assigned a moral meaning, ordinary ambiguity becomes intolerable.

Thought-action fusion does not need to be argued away in real time. If you turn every intrusion into a debate about whether thoughts equal actions, the debate can become another compulsion. The more useful move is to recognize the rule and decline the assignment.

"I notice my mind is treating a thought as evidence."

Then return to the behavior that matters.

Responsibility Has a Limit

Fatherhood requires responsibility. Babies genuinely need adults to prevent hazards they cannot understand. You use a car seat correctly. You hold a child on stairs. You keep medication out of reach. You supervise water. You follow medical advice when a child is ill.

OCD does not usually oppose responsibility. It expands it until there is no reasonable stopping point.

The distinction can be seen in one ordinary scene. A father checks that the stair gate has latched. That is normal safety. Then he pulls it again because the first check did not feel certain. Then he photographs it before leaving the room. Then he returns to compare the photograph with the physical gate. The external risk did not change. The standard of internal certainty did.

Inflated responsibility is the belief that you must prevent an outcome at a level beyond ordinary human control. New parenthood can make this belief unusually persuasive because the stakes are real. Nobody wants to say, "Be less responsible about your baby."

So do not use that phrase.

Ask instead, "What would reasonable responsibility look like if I were not trying to erase every possibility?"

Reasonable responsibility has an endpoint. The car seat is fastened according to instructions. The medication is stored. The bath is supervised. The action can be completed.

Compulsive responsibility has no endpoint because the target is a feeling of certainty.

The Certainty Trap

Darius made himself a promise. He would carry his son downstairs again as soon as he knew the thought did not mean anything.

The promise sounded temporary.

Two weeks later, his partner was still doing the stairs.

This is the certainty trap: life is postponed until a question receives an answer that the question itself is designed to reject. "Can I know with complete confidence that I will never lose control?" "Can I prove that a sensation meant nothing?" "Can I be certain I am different from every dangerous person I have ever read about?"

The mind treats these questions as if they are difficult but solvable. That is why hours of checking can feel productive. The person is not choosing to waste time. He believes the next piece of evidence may finally close the case.

The case keeps changing its burden of proof.

Suppose your partner says, "I trust you." The mind asks whether she knows everything. You tell her more. She still trusts you. The mind asks whether love has biased her judgment. You ask a clinician. The clinician explains intrusive thoughts. The mind asks whether you described your thought accurately enough. You search online. The mind finds an exception.

A certainty-seeking system can convert reassurance into new material indefinitely.

The way out is not a stronger answer. It is a different goal.

A More Useful Goal

The goal is not "I will feel sure."

The goal is "I will choose ordinary responsible behavior even when my mind cannot give me perfect certainty."

That sentence can sound weak to somebody in the middle of an obsession. It feels as though you are accepting danger.

You are accepting uncertainty, which is different.

All parenting contains uncertainty. A careful father cannot guarantee that his toddler will never trip. A loving father cannot guarantee he will never become frustrated. A competent father cannot promise that every medical decision will be perfect.

Responsibility means using available information and appropriate safeguards, not possessing knowledge humans do not have.

OCD takes the ordinary sentence "I cannot guarantee everything" and translates it into "Then you are willing to let harm happen."

That translation is false, but do not spend all evening proving it false. Notice what it is asking you to do.

Usually it is asking for another compulsion.

The Feelings Test

One of the crueler forms of checking is emotional checking.

A father has a disturbing thought and immediately measures disgust. Was it strong enough? He notices that he feels numb after weeks of anxiety. Does numbness mean agreement? He laughs at something unrelated ten minutes later. How could he laugh if the thought truly horrified him? He sees his baby after a difficult day and feels tired instead of flooded with love. Does that reveal something?

No emotion can perform the job being assigned to it.

Feelings vary with sleep, stress, hunger, repetition, context, and attention. A thought that produced a jolt on Monday may produce less on Friday simply because it has become familiar. If distress is being used as evidence of morality, reduced distress can become frightening.

That creates a trap. You want the thought to bother you less because the anxiety is exhausting. Then, when it bothers you less, you worry that you have stopped caring.

This is one reason symptom improvement can itself become an obsessional trigger.

You do not need to force disgust back into place. You do not need to test affection. You do not need to stare at your baby until you feel the "right" amount of warmth.

Feelings are experiences. They are not sworn testimony.

A Small Experiment in Not Knowing

Choose a mild certainty question, not the most frightening one in your life.

It might be, "Did I check the bottle lid carefully enough?" or "Was I too impatient during that nappy change?"

Notice the usual route. Do you replay? Ask your partner? Search? Return to inspect? Make a promise to be more careful?

For a short period, delay one of those responses.

Do not replace it with a new reassurance sentence such as, "Everything is definitely fine." Try something closer to, "I have checked in the ordinary way, and I am not going to solve the feeling of doubt right now."

Then do the next concrete task.

This is not full ERP. It is an observation exercise. You are learning what the urge to obtain certainty feels like and how quickly it tries to recruit behavior.

You may discover that doubt rises when you do not respond. That does not mean the response was necessary. It means the response had been regulating the feeling.

If the exercise concerns genuine safety, complex symptoms, or a situation where you are not sure what ordinary practice is, do not improvise. Ask a qualified professional or use established childcare guidance. OCD treatment does not require abandoning normal safety.

Darius and the Banister

Darius eventually talked to a therapist who treated OCD. They did not spend the first session deciding whether his staircase thought had been "really" an urge. The therapist was more interested in what happened after it.

Darius described the avoidance. He described the memory review. He described asking his partner whether she ever had thoughts like his. He described reading news stories about parents who harmed children and comparing his emotions with the people in the articles.

The therapist helped him see that he had built a system around one impossible goal: know yourself with enough certainty that no future action can surprise you.

A reasonable father knows his values, his history, his behavior, and his current intentions. He can make responsible choices from those. He cannot obtain a metaphysical guarantee about every future second of his life.

Darius's early treatment work included carrying his son in ordinary situations while reducing extra checking and review. The details were individualized and supervised. The key learning was not "stairs are safe." Stairs require normal care. The learning was, "I can use normal care without turning my mind into a second stair gate."

That line stayed with him because it gave responsibility a boundary.

Moral Perfection Is Not the Same as Good Fathering

A father can become so concerned with proving goodness that he stops practicing it.

Good fathering is behavioral. You feed, comfort, protect, apologize, play, repair, learn, show up, and get help when you need it. None of those actions requires a perfectly clean stream of consciousness.

Moral perfection is a different project. It asks you never to think the wrong thing, never to feel the wrong emotion, never to have an ambiguous sensation, and never to make a mistake that could be misinterpreted later.

That project has no finish line.

The distinction matters especially with taboo thoughts. If goodness is measured by mental content, the father becomes a full-time monitor of the one place he can never completely control. If goodness is practiced through behavior and responsibility, he can notice the thought and return to what his child actually needs.

The child does not need a father who wins every argument with his mind.

The child needs a father who can stay in the room.

When Logic Becomes Another Ritual

There is a difference between learning a useful idea and using the idea compulsively.

After reading about thought-action fusion, a father may start labeling every disturbing thought: "That is thought-action fusion. Therefore the thought is meaningless. Therefore I am safe." If the label has to be repeated until anxiety drops, it has stopped being simple education and started functioning like reassurance.

This matters because smart people can build sophisticated compulsions. They do not merely say, "I am okay." They quote diagnostic criteria, compare probabilities, search journal articles, or run philosophical arguments about free will. The language changes. The job stays the same: make uncertainty disappear.

Education should widen your choices. A ritual narrows them.

A useful test is to ask what happens if you do not finish the argument. Can you notice the concept, leave the conclusion unresolved, and return to the nappy, the dishes, the walk, or the conversation? If not, the mind may be using knowledge as another checking tool.

Owen discovered this after reading several OCD articles. He had begun to feel safer only when he could explain his fear in the "correct" clinical terms. Then a new thought appeared that did not fit the example he had read. He panicked, not because the content was objectively worse, but because his reassurance system had lost a category.

His clinician gave him a less elegant task: stop categorizing every thought.

The work was frustrating. It was also freeing. He could understand the general process without making diagnostic certainty a prerequisite for breakfast.

Use the ideas in this book the same way. Learn them well enough to recognize a pattern. Then let them point you toward behavior, assessment, and treatment rather than another private trial.

Action Challenge: Find the Hidden Standard

Complete this sentence once:

"I will allow myself to do this parenting task when I am certain that __________."

Read what you wrote.

Can a human being ever meet that standard? Is it a normal safety standard, such as following the manufacturer's car-seat instructions, or an internal-certainty standard, such as knowing beyond doubt what a thought means?

If it is a normal safety standard, keep it.

If it is an impossible certainty standard, do not immediately force yourself into the feared situation. Bring the standard to your treatment planning. Ask what ordinary responsibility would look like and what extra behavior the certainty trap has added.

The purpose is not to make you fearless. It is to make the rule visible.

In a Nutshell

Thought-action fusion makes mental content feel like moral or predictive evidence. Inflated responsibility tells you that a good father should eliminate possibilities no human can eliminate. The certainty trap keeps ordinary life on hold until the impossible standard is met.

The response is not careless parenting. It is ordinary responsibility with an endpoint.

Check what needs checking. Follow real safety guidance. Take behavior seriously. Then notice when the task changes from caring for your child to proving something unprovable about your mind.

You do not have to feel certain to act responsibly.

Chapter 4: Avoidance Can Look Like Good Parenting

Ethan became known in his house as the bottle guy.

He washed them before anybody asked. He measured formula carefully. He kept the drying rack organized. At night, when the baby woke, Ethan would get up first and bring everything to his partner.

He looked involved because he was involved.

What he did not do was change nappies.

At first the reason was easy to hide. His partner had more practice. Ethan was slow. The baby cried when he did it. Then a taboo intrusive thought appeared during a change, and the task acquired a new meaning. Ethan did not merely dislike the thought. He concluded that avoiding the situation was part of protecting his child.

The bottle role expanded. The nappy role disappeared.

His partner interpreted the imbalance as selective competence: Ethan somehow found energy for the jobs he preferred and helplessness for the ones he did not. Ethan interpreted her frustration as evidence that disclosure would make things worse. He worked harder at bottles.

This is what makes avoidance so easy to miss. It can wear the clothes of responsibility.

What Avoidance Is Trying to Do

Avoidance means not entering, leaving, delaying, delegating, or altering a situation in order to reduce distress or prevent a feared outcome. In OCD, avoidance can function as a compulsion. The International OCD Foundation's perinatal OCD material specifically lists avoiding holding a baby, bathing a baby, spending time alone with a baby, and using feared objects or places among possible compulsive responses (International OCD Foundation, n.d.).

The word possible matters. Not every refusal is OCD.

A father may not do bath time because his shift ends late. He may avoid carrying a child on stairs because he has a genuine balance problem. A family may divide tasks according to preference, culture, breastfeeding, disability, work, or simple efficiency. Behavior has to be understood in context.

The useful question is function: what is the behavior trying to accomplish?

Ethan's nappy avoidance was trying to prevent a feared moral catastrophe and eliminate uncertainty about himself. The same outward behavior could have had a completely different function in another family.

Once you ask about function, the pattern becomes easier to see.

The Safety Argument

Avoidance usually comes with a strong argument.

"Why take a chance?"

It is a powerful sentence because nobody wants to be the person arguing for unnecessary risk with a baby.

The problem is that "chance" can mean two very different things. It can mean a real, identifiable hazard that normal safety practice addresses. Or it can mean the existence of uncertainty itself.

Normal safety says, "Do not leave an infant unattended in a bath."

OCD-style safety may say, "Do not be the person giving the bath because you once had a thought."

Normal safety says, "Use knives carefully and store them appropriately."

OCD-style safety may say, "Do not prepare food while your child is in the house because the presence of a knife plus a thought creates unacceptable uncertainty."

Normal safety has rules that other reasonable adults can recognize. Compulsive safety tends to become private, expandable, and dependent on how you feel.

That does not make the father foolish. It means fear has taken a legitimate value, child safety, and changed the standard.

The Learning Avoidance Prevents

When you avoid a feared task, you often feel immediate relief.

That relief is informative. It shows you why avoidance is so sticky.

Imagine a father who feels intense anxiety when alone with his baby. His partner takes over. Anxiety drops. The nervous system learns a simple sequence: solo care was dangerous; escape made the danger feeling stop.

The father may interpret the relief as proof that leaving was correct.

What he does not get to learn is what would have happened if he had remained in an ordinary, appropriate care situation without performing the escape or another compulsion.

In exposure and response prevention, the learning comes from contact with feared cues or situations while reducing the rituals used to neutralize distress. NICE includes CBT with ERP among recommended treatments for OCD (National Institute for Health and Care Excellence, 2005). In perinatal OCD literature, avoidance of infant-care situations has been described as a treatment target in maternal cases (Hudak & Wisner, 2012).

Father-specific treatment trials are limited. We should not pretend otherwise. The treatment principles come from OCD evidence more broadly, with perinatal examples helping illustrate how those principles can apply around childcare.

The lesson is not "force yourself to do everything." The lesson is that repeated escape has a learning effect of its own.

The Partner Pays for Private Safety Rules

Avoidance rarely stays private in a household with a baby.

If you do not do the bath, somebody else does. If you cannot be alone with the child, somebody else cannot leave. If you avoid stairs, somebody else carries. If you will not use kitchen utensils while the baby is nearby, meal preparation changes.

This is not a reason to shame a frightened father. Shame is already abundant and rarely makes behavior more flexible.

It is a reason to count the cost honestly.

Ethan believed he was protecting his daughter. His partner was doing every nappy change and beginning to resent him. Both facts belonged in the treatment picture. A mental-health explanation can create understanding. It does not erase workload.

One useful conversation separates two subjects that often get tangled.

Subject one is the OCD-style process: thoughts, fear, avoidance, checking, reassurance.

Subject two is the practical division of care: who is doing what, how often, and at what cost.

If every workload discussion becomes a debate about whether the father is dangerous, the family gets nowhere. If every mental-health discussion becomes an argument about chores, the father may retreat further into secrecy.

Separate the conversations so each can be solved on its own terms.

The Clever Forms of Avoidance

Avoidance is not always a flat refusal.

It can be timing. You take a shower exactly when the baby usually needs changing.

It can be substitution. You volunteer for grocery runs because the shops feel safer than staying home alone with the baby.

It can be positioning. You sit on the floor instead of the sofa because you fear dropping the child, even when the child is secure.

It can be equipment. You add unnecessary layers of barriers, gloves, monitoring, or special arrangements that reduce contact with the trigger.

It can be social. You invite someone over every time your partner leaves.

It can be cognitive. You do the task physically while trying not to notice the baby, suppressing thoughts, repeating a phrase, or mentally reviewing every movement.

That last category matters. A father can appear fully involved while an internal compulsion makes the task exhausting.

If you only count visible avoidance, you may miss how much energy is going into "being there safely."

Not Every Boundary Should Be Broken

A book about avoidance can create pressure to treat every limit as fear.

Do not do that.

You are allowed to have preferences. You are allowed to divide labor. You are allowed to decline tasks because of pain, disability, exhaustion, religious practice, work, or other real constraints. You are allowed to set boundaries in a relationship. You are allowed to use normal safety tools and follow medical advice.

The question is not whether you do every parenting task.

The question is whether fear and certainty-seeking are deciding which tasks you are permitted to do, especially when you would otherwise want to participate.

That distinction is central to the Stay-In Ladder.

Ethan did not secretly hate nappy changes more than the average parent. He wanted to help. He wanted the easy physical closeness that sometimes came with changing and dressing his daughter. He had removed himself because the task triggered a moral threat.

That makes it a good candidate for assessment and, if appropriate, treatment work.

Build an Avoidance Inventory

Do this exercise in prose rather than as a scorecard.

Choose three situations you have changed since the thoughts became a problem.

For each, write the ordinary task first. "Change a nappy." "Carry the baby downstairs." "Be home alone for an hour."

Then write the feared meaning. Not merely the event. The meaning might be, "If I have the thought while doing this, I cannot trust myself," or, "If I feel anxious near the stairs, that proves I am unsafe."

Then write the current response. "I delegate." "I wait until my partner is home." "I use extra checks." "I leave the room."

Finally, write the cost. Include the cost to you and, if relevant, to somebody else.

Do not rank the situations yet. Do not force re-entry before you understand whether normal safety or other clinical issues need to be considered. The inventory is for seeing the footprint of avoidance.

A useful question is: if the intrusive thought vanished tomorrow, which of these tasks would I want back?

The answer often reveals where fear has been making decisions.

A Failed Re-Entry

Ethan tried to fix the problem on a Saturday.

His partner was tired and angry. Ethan was tired of feeling ashamed. He announced that he would do every nappy change that day.

The first went badly. His anxiety rose. He monitored every sensation. He rushed through the task and immediately asked his partner, "Did that seem normal to you?"

She said yes.

He asked again ten minutes later.

By lunchtime, Ethan decided the experiment had proved he was not ready.

This is a common mistake. He changed the visible avoidance but kept the internal system intact. He was still using monitoring and reassurance to produce certainty. He had also chosen an all-day test that turned every care task into an exam.

Exposure-based work is not a test of whether you can feel calm. It is practice in responding differently to fear and uncertainty. The structure matters.

A smaller re-entry would have given him more information. One ordinary change. Normal hygiene. No special body-monitoring. Delay the reassurance question. Finish the task. Let the emotional result be whatever it is.

Because the situation involved a child and taboo content, Ethan later planned his steps with an OCD-trained clinician. That was appropriate. Self-help should not become improvised treatment when risk is unclear or symptoms are severe.

The Difference Between "Cannot" and "Will Not"

Language can expose how avoidance has hardened.

"I cannot do bath time" sounds like a permanent fact.

"I am avoiding bath time because it triggers a fear I do not know how to handle" describes a current behavior and a reason.

The second sentence does not force you to act. It gives you room to act later.

Try this with one avoided task. Replace "I can't" with a description of what happens.

"I am avoiding being alone with my daughter because the intrusive thoughts get louder and I seek reassurance."

"I am avoiding the kitchen when my son is nearby because knives trigger harm obsessions."

"I am avoiding nappies because taboo thoughts make me monitor my reactions."

Specific language is useful because treatment works on patterns, not identities.

"Dangerous father" is an identity claim.

"Avoidance followed by reassurance" is a pattern.

Patterns can be observed, discussed, and changed.

When Normal Safety Is Unclear

New fathers often have genuine uncertainty about what is normal childcare safety. That creates a problem for OCD work because you need a reasonable baseline.

Use reliable childcare guidance and qualified professionals for factual safety questions. Ask the pediatrician how to supervise a bath. Follow the car-seat manufacturer's instructions. Use established safe-sleep guidance. Get medical advice for feeding, medication, or developmental concerns.

Then resist turning one answer into a repeated certainty ritual.

A factual question has an endpoint. You learn the relevant rule and apply it.

A compulsive question changes after the rule is known: "But what if I am the exception?" "What if I misunderstood?" "What if the guidance does not account for my thought?"

The first question belongs in education. The second set may belong in OCD treatment.

Ethan Gets One Task Back

Ethan's first successful re-entry was intentionally unremarkable.

He changed his daughter's nappy while his partner was in the next room. He used the same hygiene and safety routine any caregiver would use. A taboo thought appeared. His anxiety rose. He noticed the urge to check his body and the urge to call his partner into the room.

He completed the change.

Afterward he did not feel triumphant. He felt unsettled.

That was useful.

The old rule said participation was permitted only when certainty arrived. Ethan had participated without it.

He repeated the task later in the week. The point was not to manufacture confidence. The point was to stop teaching his mind that the nappy table was a place he could enter only under special mental conditions.

The bottle rack did not disappear. He still liked being the bottle guy.

He was no longer using bottles to stay away from being a father in another part of the room.

The False Economy of Delegation

Avoidance can look efficient because it removes distress from one moment. The family pays later.

If your partner always handles the trigger, you do not only lose practice. The partner loses flexibility. A simple errand becomes a scheduling problem. A night out becomes impossible. Illness or travel turns one person's fear into everybody's logistics.

That does not mean a partner should withdraw support suddenly. Accommodation can be changed gradually, and a clinician can help families decide what is appropriate. The point is to see the economic truth of the arrangement: fear has been receiving labor from more than one person.

When you count the cost of an avoidance compulsion, count minutes, missed tasks, resentment, planning burden, and the experiences you are no longer sharing. Cost is not punishment. It is information about whether the current strategy is actually protecting the family you meant to protect.

Principles to Remember

Avoidance can be a compulsion when its function is to reduce obsessional fear or obtain certainty. The same outward behavior can also have ordinary reasons, so function matters.

Count the cost without using shame. A private safety rule can redistribute childcare, restrict a partner's freedom, and remove you from tasks you actually value.

Re-entry is not a dare and not an argument against real safety. Use normal childcare guidance. Work with a qualified professional when symptoms are severe, taboo content is involved, or risk is unclear. The aim is to reduce the extra rules fear has added to ordinary care.

You do not need to do every job. You do need to know who is choosing the jobs you have stopped doing.

PART II: THE LOOPS THAT PULL YOU OUT

Certainty, anger, disclosure, taboo themes, and the retreat from care.

Chapter 5: The Good-Dad Certainty Trap

Farid's phone knew the search before he finished typing.

The first few times he had looked for information about intrusive thoughts, he found useful material. He learned that OCD can involve violent or taboo obsessions. He learned that people can perform mental compulsions as well as visible ones. He found language that made his experience less mysterious.

Then the search changed jobs.

Instead of learning, Farid began checking.

He searched variations of the same question late at night. He read clinical pages, forums, news stories, and comment threads. He compared his exact wording with strangers' exact wording. If another father described a thought that sounded like his, Farid felt relief. If the example differed, he wondered whether the difference was significant.

He also checked himself. Had he looked at his son normally? Had he felt the right amount of warmth during story time? Had a moment of irritation lasted too long? Did the fact that he had stopped feeling shocked by a repeated thought mean he was getting used to it?

The phone was only one tool. The real search engine was in his head.

The Good-Dad Standard

A value can become a compulsion when it is turned into a demand for proof.

Farid wanted to be a good father. That is not a symptom. The problem began when "good father" stopped describing a pattern of behavior and became a state he had to verify internally.

How do you prove you are a good father?

You can point to actions. You care for your child. You apologize when you get something wrong. You follow ordinary safety guidance. You seek help when a problem is interfering with family life.

OCD asks for a different kind of proof. It wants certainty about motive, character, future behavior, and hidden desire. It asks you to confirm that every emotion is compatible with goodness and every thought is sufficiently rejected.

That test can be failed by anything.

You are affectionate. Perhaps you are overcompensating.

You feel tired. Perhaps you do not love your child enough.

You are frustrated. Perhaps anger reveals danger.

You are calm around a thought that once terrified you. Perhaps calmness means agreement.

The standard is not designed to measure behavior. It is designed to keep the question open.

Reassurance Is Not Always Spoken

Most people recognize reassurance when it sounds like this: "Tell me I would never do that."

The more sophisticated forms can hide.

A father tells his partner a detailed story about the thought but quietly waits for her facial expression. If she looks relaxed, relief arrives. If she pauses, the pause becomes evidence.

A father asks, "Do other dads ever get weird thoughts?" The question sounds educational. He asks it five times in different forms because he wants the answer to settle his own case.

A father reads a book sentence stating that intrusive thoughts can occur in OCD, then rereads it whenever anxiety rises.

A father checks whether he still feels distressed by a taboo image. Distress itself becomes reassurance.

A father prays, repeats a moral phrase, or mentally lists reasons he loves his child until his internal state feels safe.

The reassurance loop is defined by function, not format. It tries to remove uncertainty now.

There is nothing morally wrong with wanting reassurance. Humans comfort each other. Partners naturally say, "I know you." Clinicians provide information. The trouble begins when reassurance is assigned a job it cannot keep: certify the future or permanently settle an obsessional doubt.

Memory Review

Mental review deserves special attention because nobody else can see it.

After a care task, you replay what happened. Where was your hand? How hard did you hold the baby? What did you feel when the crying started? Did the thought come before the irritation or after? Did you move away because you were afraid, or did fear come after you noticed the movement?

A single reflection can be reasonable. Repeated review often makes memory less satisfying, not more.

Memory is not a video file. Attention selects details. Repetition changes what feels familiar. Anxiety can make gaps more salient. The more exact the standard becomes, the more ordinary uncertainty looks suspicious.

Farid once spent forty minutes reconstructing a two-second interaction at the changing table. By the end, he was less certain than when he began.

That outcome did not teach him to stop. It taught him to review more carefully next time.

This is how a compulsion gains authority: failure is interpreted as evidence that the dose was insufficient.

Confession Can Become a Ritual

Honest disclosure is often important. Compulsive confession is different.

A useful disclosure gives enough information for a partner or clinician to understand the problem and respond appropriately.

Compulsive confession seeks moral cleansing.

The father feels a spike of doubt and tells his partner the thought. Relief comes when the partner reacts kindly. A new detail occurs to him. He adds it. Then he worries that leaving out a sensation was dishonest. He confesses that too.

Soon the partner is being asked to evaluate a stream of mental events neither person can resolve.

The distinction is especially important with taboo content. A father may believe complete honesty requires reporting every variation. In treatment, that level of detail may not be necessary. A clinician can help determine what information matters for assessment and what functions as a ritual.

Ask yourself what you are requesting when you disclose. Understanding? Practical support? Clinical assessment? Or a verdict that you remain a good person?

The first three can lead somewhere. The last tends to expire.

Internet Research: When Learning Ends

The internet can save time and reduce isolation. It can also create a perfect checking environment because the supply of information has no natural endpoint.

A useful research session has a question that can be answered.

"What kind of therapy is recommended for OCD?"

"What credentials or experience should I ask a clinician about?"

"What are the current safe-sleep recommendations from a reliable medical source?"

Once you have a trustworthy answer, the task can end.

Compulsive research has a different structure.

"Can I find one description that matches my thought exactly?"

"Can I prove that nobody who had this sensation ever acted on it?"

"Can I read enough cases to know I am not an exception?"

The first type gathers information for a decision. The second type asks a database to remove uncertainty from human life.

No database can.

If you notice yourself opening the same tabs after midnight, do not shame yourself for "doomscrolling." Ask what verdict you are trying to extract.

Comparing Yourself With Dangerous People

Harm obsessions can pull a father toward news stories about people who have harmed children. He may read for clues.

Did that person seek help? Did they say they loved their child? Were they anxious? Did they have intrusive thoughts? Did they sleep badly? Did they appear normal to friends?

Every human similarity can become frightening because the comparison has an impossible purpose: identify a feature that separates "safe people" from "dangerous people" with complete certainty.

The exercise ignores base rates, context, diagnosis, intent, behavior, and the enormous complexity of real cases. More importantly, it turns tragedy into a private sorting machine.

Stop using news stories as diagnostic tests.

If you need a risk assessment, obtain one from a qualified professional who can evaluate you directly. If you are reading cases to reduce obsessional doubt, bring that behavior into treatment like any other compulsion.

You do not need to solve yourself through strangers.

Delay, Do Not Debate

Farid's first practical change was not "never search again." That would have turned the phone into a forbidden object and created another absolute rule.

He delayed.

When the urge to search appeared, he wrote the search phrase in a note and waited twenty minutes. During the wait he completed whatever ordinary task had been interrupted.

The first evening he wrote six phrases.

By the end of twenty minutes, he still wanted to search three of them. He discussed the pattern with his therapist. Together they worked on reducing reassurance-seeking and internet checking as part of his OCD treatment.

The delay taught Farid something. An urge could be noticed without immediate obedience.

This is a useful self-observation practice for mild certainty behaviors. It is not a requirement to tolerate a genuine safety question. If your child needs medical advice, get medical advice. If you are unsure about a real childcare rule, use a reliable source. The skill is learning to recognize when the factual question has already been answered and the mind has changed the task.

The Partner's Face

Farid's partner, Leila, had become part of the checking system without agreeing to it.

Farid would say something like, "I had a strange moment during bedtime." Then he watched her.

If she kept stirring the pasta, relief. If she stopped stirring, alarm.

Leila eventually told him, "I feel like every expression I make becomes evidence."

That sentence mattered because it identified a form of reassurance nobody had named.

Farid was not only asking questions. He was reading his partner.

He began practicing a different disclosure: state what happened functionally, say what support he wanted, and stop monitoring for a verdict.

"I had the intrusive-thought loop during bedtime and I want you to know I am working on not reviewing it. I do not need you to tell me what it means. Can we talk about who is doing bedtime tomorrow?"

The first few times, that felt almost rude. He was used to emotional certainty as proof of honesty.

In fact, the new conversation made more room for the relationship.

Action Challenge: Identify One Certainty Behavior

Choose one behavior that has a clear certainty function.

Do not choose every compulsion at once. Pick one that is frequent and low enough in risk that delaying it is reasonable.

Name the trigger.

Name the behavior.

Name the promised result.

For example: "After a taboo thought during a nappy change, I ask my partner whether I seemed normal. The promised result is certainty that the thought says nothing about me."

Then ask whether the result lasts.

If it does not, you have useful information.

Work with your clinician on whether the next step is delaying the behavior, reducing it, or practicing response prevention in another way. The goal is not to punish yourself by withholding comfort. The goal is to stop giving one short-lived strategy authority over the entire evening.

When Reassurance Is Appropriate

There are times when reassurance is ordinary and humane.

A partner says, "The doctor said the fever is expected after the vaccine."

A friend says, "You made a reasonable choice."

A clinician explains that a symptom is common in OCD.

Information and comfort are not banned.

The question is whether you can receive them once and continue with life, or whether the answer has to be repeated, refined, and tested until it produces a particular feeling.

Compulsion is not defined by kindness. It is defined by the loop.

This distinction prevents an OCD book from becoming rigid. You do not need to treat every supportive sentence as dangerous. You do need to notice when support has become a machine for certainty.

Farid Puts the Phone Down

One night, Farid's son woke at 2:10. After settling him, Farid had an intrusive doubt about a moment from earlier in the day.

His hand moved toward the phone.

He stopped.

The old plan would have been to search until he found a father whose story matched his. The new plan was less satisfying. He wrote one line in the note: "Urge to search whether reduced disgust means danger."

Then he put the phone face down.

His anxiety did not vanish. He lay awake for a while.

The next morning, the question still existed, but it no longer owned three hours of the night.

He discussed it in treatment. The therapist was interested in the reduced-disgust checking, not in delivering a final interpretation of the thought.

Farid slowly learned that a good father could be a person who did not answer every question his fear produced.

That was a more demanding standard than certainty.

It was also one he could practice.

A Better Use for Measurement

OCD loves measurement when the number is supposed to prove safety. Measurement becomes more useful when it tracks behavior instead.

Do not score how dangerous you felt. Count how many times you asked the same reassurance question. Do not rate whether your love felt strong enough. Notice how many care tasks you avoided. Do not calculate the probability that a thought could come true. Record how much sleep you lost to checking.

Behavioral measurement gives you something treatment can work with.

Farid kept a simple tally for one week. He did not write the content of every thought. He marked only three things: reassurance requests, internet-checking sessions, and care tasks he handed over because of obsessional doubt. The numbers were not used to shame him. They showed him that the problem occupied more of the week than he had realized.

They also gave his therapist a baseline.

A month later, Farid still had intrusive thoughts. The tally had changed. Fewer searches. Fewer reassurance questions. More bedtime participation.

If he had measured recovery by whether the thoughts had disappeared, he would have called the month a failure. Measuring the response told a different story.

That is a useful correction to the good-dad test. You cannot reliably grade character by inspecting internal noise. You can observe whether fear is taking over your behavior and whether treatment is helping you take that behavior back.

A single bad day does not invalidate the measure. Look for direction across weeks, not a perfect line. If the tally itself becomes something you check compulsively, stop using it and tell your clinician. A tool that was meant to create perspective should not become another courtroom.

Principles to Remember

The good-dad certainty trap turns a value into a proof requirement. Reassurance, memory review, confession, internet research, comparison, and emotional checking can all serve the same function: remove doubt now.

Useful information has an endpoint. A certainty ritual changes the question after the answer arrives.

Do not ban comfort or learning. Notice the job you are asking them to do.

A good father is not a person who can prove his mind is pure. He is a person who can practice responsible behavior, repair mistakes, seek help, and remain involved without requiring a permanent verdict first.

Chapter 6: Anger, Shutdown, and the Second Story

Gabriel had been awake in pieces for three nights.

His son was teething. The crying came in waves, and every attempt to settle him seemed to work for twelve minutes. At 4:40 in the morning, Gabriel carried the baby into the kitchen, realized he had left the bottle upstairs, and swore loudly.

His partner appeared in the doorway.

"Give him to me," she said.

Gabriel handed over the baby immediately. Nobody was hurt. He stood alone in the kitchen, ashamed of how sharp his voice had sounded.

Then the second story began.

If I can get that angry, maybe the harm thoughts are warnings.

For the next week, Gabriel avoided being alone with his son whenever he was tired. He was not only frightened of anger. He was using anger as evidence in an OCD-style case against himself.

The anger deserved attention. So did the case he built from it. They were related, but they were not the same problem.

Anger Is Behavior and Information, Not a Diagnosis

The supplied book idea proposed that paternal intrusive-thought problems may "come out as anger." That wording goes further than the current father-specific OCD evidence supports.

Research on paternal perinatal depression does describe irritability, anger, and frustration in some fathers. In one qualitative study of eight fathers with postpartum depression, feelings of inadequacy and powerlessness sometimes turned into anger and frustration (Pedersen et al., 2021). Broader work on paternal help-seeking also shows that fathers can face stigma and difficulty recognizing their own mental-health symptoms (Reay et al., 2024).

Those findings matter. They do not establish anger as a characteristic male presentation of harm OCD.

A father can be angry and have OCD. He can be depressed and have OCD. He can be sleep-deprived, resentful, traumatized, using substances, overwhelmed, or in relationship conflict. He can also behave aggressively without having any of those conditions. A single label cannot responsibly absorb every form of paternal distress.

This is important because two mistakes sit on either side.

The first mistake is moral panic: "I raised my voice, therefore the intrusive thought is true."

The second mistake is medical excuse: "My mental health made me angry, therefore my behavior does not count."

Neither is useful.

The Behavior Still Counts

If you shout, throw objects, punch walls, drive dangerously, handle a child roughly, frighten your partner, or feel you may lose control, deal with the behavior directly.

Put the child in a safe place or transfer care to a safe adult if you are becoming overwhelmed. Remove yourself from an escalating argument when that can be done safely. Seek professional help for anger, depression, substance use, trauma, or other problems that may be present. If you fear you may act violently, have a plan, or cannot keep people safe, seek urgent in-person help.

This is not the place for an exposure exercise.

OCD treatment asks people to reduce compulsive avoidance of ordinary situations. It does not ask a person to remain in a situation when there is an active, credible risk of harmful behavior.

That distinction protects both sides of the problem.

Gabriel's therapist did not tell him to ignore the kitchen incident. They talked about sleep, anger, and safe handover when overwhelmed. They also examined the obsessional process that followed: one episode of swearing became evidence that he should never be trusted while tired.

The first plan addressed behavior. The second plan addressed the meaning and avoidance.

Sleep Makes Everything Harder Without Explaining Everything

Newborn sleep disruption is not a diagnosis. It is a context that can make emotion regulation, concentration, and distress tolerance harder.

A father who has slept badly may feel more irritable. He may have a shorter attention span. Intrusive thoughts can feel stickier because he has fewer mental resources available to redirect attention. He may also become more rigid about routines because unpredictability feels harder to tolerate.

None of that tells you what a specific thought means.

The temptation is to use sleep as either a complete explanation or a complete dismissal.

"These thoughts are only because I am tired."

"Because I had the thought even when rested, it must be real."

Both sentences ask sleep to settle a question it cannot settle.

Use sleep information for practical care. Share night work where possible. Ask for help. Discuss severe insomnia with a clinician, especially if it appears alongside agitation, racing thoughts, unusual energy, confusion, psychotic symptoms, or mood changes. Treat sleep as part of the clinical picture, not as a morality test.

Shutdown Can Also Be a Response

Not every distressed father becomes visibly irritable.

Some become quiet.

They go to work early. They stay in the shower longer. They scroll. They volunteer for errands. They stop initiating contact with the baby because contact has become a trigger. Their partner may interpret the absence as lack of interest.

Hugo, before the disclosure described in the next chapter, did this for weeks. He was courteous and useful. He also made sure he was never the only adult in the room with his daughter.

Shutdown can arise from many causes. In an OCD loop, it can function as avoidance. In depression, it may reflect low mood, anhedonia, exhaustion, or hopelessness. In relationship conflict, it can be withdrawal. In trauma, it may have another function.

The outward behavior does not diagnose the mechanism.

Ask what happens immediately before the withdrawal, what relief it produces, and what else is happening in mood, sleep, energy, pleasure, substance use, and functioning. Those answers belong in a professional assessment when the problem is persistent or significant.

The Second Story

The first story is the event.

"I was angry."

"I felt numb."

"I wanted the crying to stop."

"I did not feel bonded to my baby for an hour."

The second story is the interpretation.

"Good fathers do not feel this."

"If I can feel this, the intrusive thought must be a warning."

"If I am relieved when somebody else takes the baby, I must not love him."

That second story often recruits checking and avoidance.

A father notices relief when his partner takes over after a hard stretch. Relief is ordinary. Caregiving is demanding. The obsessional interpretation says relief proves he wanted to escape the child, not just the difficult moment. He monitors the next handover. Now even relief is suspicious.

Mental life becomes crowded with evidence.

You do not need to approve of every feeling. You need to stop treating feelings as a hidden risk instrument.

Behavior is where responsibility belongs.

A Two-Plan Approach

If anger or shutdown is part of your picture, write two plans.

The first is a behavior and safety plan.

What do you do when you are becoming overwhelmed? Who can take over? What signs tell you to step away from an argument? What behavior is unacceptable regardless of how distressed you feel? What professional help do you need if anger, depression, substance use, or other symptoms are becoming a problem?

The second is an OCD plan.

What thought follows the anger or numbness? What meaning do you assign it? What checking begins? What parenting task do you avoid afterward? What reassurance do you request?

Do not collapse the plans.

The safety plan may include leaving a situation when you are genuinely escalating. The OCD plan may include reducing avoidance in ordinary care situations when no actual escalation is occurring. A clinician can help you distinguish them if the lines feel unclear.

That is especially important around a baby. Responsible treatment is not a guessing game.

Gabriel's Rule About Tiredness

After the kitchen incident, Gabriel created a rule: he would not be alone with his son if he had slept fewer than six hours.

The rule seemed scientific. It was not based on a clinical assessment or any individualized evidence. It was an anxiety threshold disguised as a safety standard.

The first problem was practical. With an infant, six uninterrupted hours were rare. The rule effectively banned solo care.

The second problem was cognitive. Gabriel began calculating sleep. Five hours and fifty minutes felt dangerous. Six hours and five minutes felt permitted. If he woke for ten minutes at 3:00, did the count reset?

OCD loves a rule that looks objective but still requires interpretation.

Gabriel brought the rule to therapy. The therapist did not replace it with a new magic number. They separated ordinary fatigue management from obsessional certainty. If Gabriel was too exhausted or angry to care safely, he needed to hand over and rest. If he was functioning normally and the rule was being used to avoid an intrusive-thought trigger, they treated the avoidance as part of the OCD pattern.

The decision depended on current functioning, not a ritualized number.

Depression Deserves Its Own Attention

Paternal depression is not rare enough to be an afterthought in a book for new fathers.

A 2016 meta-analysis of 74 studies estimated paternal depression during pregnancy and the first year postpartum at 8.4 percent, with substantial heterogeneity across studies (Cameron et al., 2016). An earlier JAMA meta-analysis reported a pooled estimate of 10.4 percent and found a moderate association between maternal and paternal depression (Paulson & Bazemore, 2010).

Different samples and measures produce different numbers. The practical point is not to memorize a prevalence rate. It is to recognize that depression can affect fathers during the same period in which obsessional problems may appear.

If you have persistent low mood, loss of interest, hopelessness, significant guilt, appetite or sleep changes beyond what the baby schedule explains, suicidal thoughts, or major impairment, tell a qualified professional. If you have thoughts of suicide with intent or plan, seek urgent help.

Do not make OCD carry symptoms that need a separate assessment.

When Shame Makes Anger Worse

Gabriel's anger was often followed by shame. The shame then made him withdraw. The withdrawal increased the partner's workload. Her frustration increased. Gabriel felt criticized and became more defensive.

The family had a loop inside the OCD loop.

They changed it by naming behavior plainly.

Gabriel stopped saying, "I am just anxious." He said, "I raised my voice. That was not okay."

His partner stopped saying, "You clearly cannot handle the baby." She said, "When you are escalating, I need you to hand over without arguing. Outside those moments, I need us to work on the avoidance because I cannot be the default parent for every trigger."

Those sentences were harder than reassurance. They were also more useful.

Mental-health language works best when it increases accountability and access to care. It works badly when it becomes a defense against the consequences other people are carrying.

Action Challenge: Separate State From Story

The next time you notice a strong state, name it in concrete language.

"I am angry."

"I am numb."

"I am exhausted."

"I am relieved someone else took over."

Then write the story your mind adds.

"Angry means dangerous."

"Numb means I do not love my child."

"Relief means I wanted to escape fatherhood."

Do not argue with the story for twenty minutes. Ask what action follows from the actual state.

If you are angry and escalating, use your safety plan.

If you are exhausted, arrange rest where possible.

If you are depressed, seek assessment.

If the state is ordinary and the story is recruiting checking or avoidance, bring that into your OCD work.

The exercise makes room for more than one problem at a time.

What Your Partner Needs to Know

A partner does not need to become your clinician in order to respond well.

They need enough information to distinguish three situations.

The first is ordinary distress: you are tired, frustrated, or anxious but behaving safely. Here the family can use normal teamwork.

The second is an OCD-style trigger: the situation is ordinary, but a frightening thought is pushing you toward checking, reassurance, or avoidance. Here it may be useful to follow the treatment plan rather than automatically remove the trigger.

The third is an actual safety concern: you are escalating, feel out of control, have intent or a plan, are intoxicated, are losing touch with reality, or cannot provide safe care. Here the priority is safety and in-person help, not response prevention.

Those categories are not a substitute for clinical judgment. They are a communication aid.

Gabriel and his partner used them to stop having the same argument. Previously, every sign of frustration led his partner to wonder whether she should take the baby, and every handover led Gabriel to wonder whether she secretly thought he was dangerous. The handover itself became loaded.

With a shared plan, the reason for a handover could be named. "You are escalating and need ten minutes" meant something different from "OCD is asking you to escape a routine feed."

That precision reduced both moral accusation and false reassurance.

It also gave Gabriel a more adult responsibility. He had to notice his behavior before his partner noticed it for him.

Repair After a Bad Moment

A father can handle an obsessional loop well and still behave poorly sometimes. He can also manage anger well and have intrusive thoughts. Improvement is not a clean moral arc.

If you have frightened your partner or child, repair starts with the behavior. Name what you did without adding a defense. Ask what practical change is needed. Follow through.

Do not turn the apology into a request for reassurance.

"I am sorry I raised my voice. I am working on a handover plan and I will use it earlier next time" is an apology.

"Tell me you know I would never really hurt anyone" shifts the emotional work back to the person who was affected.

That distinction can feel harsh when shame is high. It is actually respectful. Your partner should not have to manage both the impact of your behavior and the OCD question about what the behavior means.

Repair is one of the most concrete forms of values-led parenting. It does not require you to prove perfection. It requires you to respond to reality.

Principles to Remember

Anger, irritability, shutdown, and numbness can occur in new fathers for many reasons. Paternal depression research gives us evidence about some of those experiences. It does not establish anger as the defining male form of harm OCD.

Take behavior seriously. Mental-health language does not excuse frightening or unsafe conduct.

At the same time, do not let one moment of irritation become proof of an obsessional fear. Separate the behavior plan from the OCD plan. Get professional help when depression, anger, substance use, trauma symptoms, sleep disruption, or safety concerns need their own assessment.

You do not need one label that explains everything. You need the right response to each thing that is actually happening.

Chapter 7: Tell Your Partner Without Making Them the Judge

Hugo's partner knew something was wrong before she knew what it was.

He had become helpful in a peculiar way. He packed the changing bag with military precision. He sterilized bottles nobody had asked him to sterilize. He checked the front door twice before bed. He offered to do the supermarket run at almost any hour.

He also stopped being alone with their daughter.

When his partner asked why, Hugo said he was anxious. That was true. He did not say what he was anxious about.

The hidden part grew heavier. An unwanted harm thought had appeared while he was holding the baby. Then another. Hugo was frightened by the content and more frightened by the possibility that saying it aloud could change how his partner saw him.

So he offered fragments.

"I keep getting weird thoughts."

"What kind of thoughts?"

"Just horrible things."

"About what?"

"I don't want to say."

His partner filled the silence with possibilities. Some were worse than the reality. Hugo watched her face and took every question as evidence that disclosure was dangerous.

By the time he finally told her more, the conversation had two years' worth of fear packed into twenty minutes.

Disclosure Has a Job

A useful disclosure is not a confession booth. It is communication for a purpose.

You may need your partner to understand why behavior has changed. You may need practical support while you arrange treatment. You may need them to attend an appointment because accommodation and reassurance have become part of the household pattern. You may simply need to stop lying about why you keep leaving the room.

Know the job before you start.

If the job is "make my partner prove I am safe," the conversation can become a reassurance ritual.

If the job is "give enough information for honesty, care planning, and assessment," there is an endpoint.

The difference changes how much detail is useful.

A partner usually does not need a graphic replay of every intrusive image. They need to know the category, that the thoughts are unwanted and distressing if that is accurate, what you do in response, how the pattern is affecting care, and what help you are seeking.

That is enough to open a real conversation.

The Four-Part Disclosure

Use four parts.

First: what happens.

"I am having repeated unwanted intrusive thoughts about harm involving the baby."

Second: what the experience is like.

"They frighten me and make me doubt myself."

Third: what you do in response.

"I have started avoiding bath time, checking my reactions, and asking you questions that are really reassurance."

Fourth: what you are asking for.

"I want an assessment from someone who understands OCD. I also want us to talk about the childcare jobs I have been avoiding."

This structure is deliberately boring. Boring is useful when the content is emotionally charged.

You are not delivering a defense speech. You are describing a pattern.

If you are unsure whether the thoughts are unwanted, if you have desire or intent to act, if there is a plan, if you are losing touch with reality, or if safety is unclear, say that directly to a qualified professional. Do not use an OCD script to force your experience into a category that does not fit.

What Your Partner May Feel

Your partner may be relieved that there is an explanation.

They may also be scared, angry, confused, skeptical, or exhausted.

Do not demand the ideal response in the first ten minutes.

A father who has spent weeks researching OCD may arrive with vocabulary his partner has never heard. He may expect immediate understanding because the clinical explanation feels obvious to him now. His partner may still be processing the sentence "I have been having thoughts about harm."

Give the conversation time without turning that time into a test.

Hugo watched his partner's eyebrows during disclosure. When she frowned, he felt a rush of panic and began talking faster. He added research. He quoted a website. He explained the difference between obsessions and intent. He asked, "You know I would never do anything, right?"

The conversation shifted from honesty to verdict.

His partner later said, "I was trying to understand, and suddenly I felt responsible for making you feel innocent."

That was the reassurance loop entering the relationship.

Family Accommodation

Family accommodation refers to ways relatives or partners change behavior to help a person avoid triggers or complete compulsions.

Accommodation can be compassionate. A partner sees distress and naturally wants to reduce it.

She takes over every bath.

She answers repeated questions.

She checks the baby monitor because he is afraid to.

She removes an ordinary household object because it triggers an obsession.

She stays home because he refuses solo care.

In the short term, everybody gets relief. In the long term, the household can become organized around the OCD.

NICE guidance notes that family or carers can sometimes be involved as co-therapists in ERP when appropriate and acceptable (National Institute for Health and Care Excellence, 2005). That does not mean a partner should invent exposure tasks or withdraw support abruptly. It means family responses can be clinically relevant and may be included in treatment planning.

A therapist can help a couple distinguish support from accommodation.

Support says, "I know this is hard, and I will help you follow the plan."

Accommodation says, "I will rearrange the world so you do not have to feel the fear."

The line can be subtle.

The Reassurance Script for Partners

A partner needs language too.

Suppose the father asks, "Do you think I am dangerous?"

A reassurance answer might be, "No, absolutely not, never, I know you better than anyone."

That may reduce distress for a few minutes. Then the father asks whether the answer would change if the partner knew another detail.

A treatment-consistent response, when a clinician has confirmed that reassurance reduction is appropriate, might sound like: "I know this is the OCD question you are working on. I am not going to judge the thought for you. I can sit with you while you follow the plan."

That sentence offers connection without a verdict.

Do not memorize it like a magic spell. Partners are not robots, and scripts can become rituals too. The point is the stance: warmth, clarity, and no promise of impossible certainty.

If there is an actual change in safety, behavior, intent, or reality testing, the response should change too. Family members should never be trained to ignore genuine warning signs in the name of avoiding reassurance.

Talk About Workload Separately

A relationship can become poisoned when every practical complaint is interpreted as a mental-health attack.

"You have not done bath time in three weeks" is a workload statement.

Hearing it as "You think I am dangerous" turns the discussion into another reassurance test.

Likewise, "I am having intrusive thoughts" is a mental-health statement.

Using it to shut down every conversation about unequal childcare turns explanation into exemption.

Separate the meetings if you have to.

One conversation can be about the OCD pattern and treatment plan.

Another can be about who does mornings, nights, feeds, baths, appointments, laundry, and solo care.

The two affect each other. They do not have to be solved in the same emotional minute.

Hugo and his partner began doing a ten-minute logistics check on Sunday afternoons. No analysis of thought content. They looked only at care tasks.

This revealed something Hugo had not wanted to see. His avoidance had turned his partner into the default parent in several high-contact jobs.

That information did not prove anything about his character.

It gave him a reason to make treatment matter.

What Not to Put on Your Partner

Your partner is not your risk assessor.

They are not your diagnostic service.

They are not required to hear every intrusive thought.

They are not responsible for getting the wording of a reassurance response exactly right.

They are also not required to carry unlimited childcare while you work on the problem.

That list may feel stern. It is meant to restore roles.

OCD can make a relationship feel like a clinic with no closing hours. One person brings evidence. The other issues verdicts. Both become exhausted.

Return the clinical work to clinicians.

Return the relationship to the things a relationship can actually do: affection, honesty, disagreement, practical teamwork, humor, sex when appropriate, meals, planning, shared fatigue, shared care, and ordinary conversation that has nothing to do with your symptoms.

You may discover how much of your time together has been consumed by the case.

The First Conversation May Go Badly

Not every disclosure becomes a tender scene.

Marcus told his partner about taboo intrusive thoughts in the car because he panicked and could not wait. She became frightened. He responded by giving too much detail. She asked him to stop. Marcus took that as confirmation that the content was unspeakable.

The next day they tried again with a clinician present.

The second conversation was shorter. The clinician asked about the unwanted nature of the thoughts, compulsions, avoidance, intent, and other safety factors. The partner learned that OCD can involve taboo content and that family accommodation can keep a cycle going. Marcus learned that his partner did not need to know every mental variation.

The first conversation had not failed because honesty was a mistake. It failed because neither person had a structure for what the information was supposed to do.

If your partner reacts strongly, do not force them to calm you. Give space. Arrange professional support. If safety is in question, prioritize assessment.

Disclosure is not a single performance you have to get right.

A Partner Can Set Limits

Partners need permission to have boundaries around reassurance.

"I will talk about treatment planning after dinner, but I am not going to answer the same safety question again tonight."

"I can take over while you call your therapist, but I cannot be the permanent solution to every avoided task."

"I will listen when you say the thought is bothering you. I do not want graphic detail."

"I need us to discuss the childcare load separately."

These are not punishments.

A boundary protects the relationship from becoming a compulsion system.

A father may initially experience the loss of reassurance as abandonment. That feeling deserves compassion. It does not automatically mean the boundary is wrong.

This is why family changes work best when they are planned rather than improvised in the middle of a spike.

Action Challenge: Plan the Conversation Before the Spike

Write your four-part disclosure when you are not in the middle of a reassurance urge.

Keep it to one paragraph.

Add one sentence about what you do not need.

"I do not need you to tell me what the thought means."

Add one sentence about practical impact.

"I have been avoiding solo care and that has put more work on you."

Add one request.

"I want us to find an OCD-informed assessment and agree on how we handle reassurance questions until then."

If the content involves safety concerns you are unsure about, make the professional contact the first request.

The goal is not elegant communication. It is honest, bounded communication.

Hugo's Evening Without the Trial

Several weeks into treatment, Hugo had an intrusive thought during bedtime.

He told his partner, "I had the loop again."

She asked, "Do you want to tell me what happened, or is that going to turn into checking?"

Hugo thought for a moment.

"I think checking."

"Okay. Do you still want to do the story?"

He did.

They read the same board book three times because their daughter demanded it. Hugo felt distracted and uncomfortable. He did not explain the thought. His partner did not certify him.

After the baby was asleep, they watched a terrible game show.

This is what recovery can look like in a relationship: not a dramatic absence of symptoms, but the return of ordinary subjects.

OCD becomes less central not because nobody cares, but because it stops chairing every meeting.

Use the Appointment to Protect the Relationship

A joint appointment can help when disclosure has tangled three questions together: What is the symptom pattern? What is an actual safety issue? What should each partner do next?

Bring a short description of the pattern rather than a transcript of every thought. Explain when it began, what situations trigger it, what you avoid, what you check, what reassurance you seek, and how much time the loop takes. Let the clinician ask for more detail where it is clinically useful.

The partner can bring a different list. Which tasks have shifted? Which reassurance questions repeat? Which routines now require special rules? What has become hard to discuss without an argument?

Those lists are often more useful than another debate at the kitchen table about what one particular thought "proves."

The appointment can also establish a shared vocabulary. Instead of saying, "You're doing the thing again," your partner can say, "Is this the reassurance loop?" Instead of saying, "You don't understand," you can say, "I think I'm asking you for certainty rather than support."

Shared language does not solve the problem by itself. It reduces the number of fights caused by two people using different maps.

If your partner does not want to attend treatment, that is not a reason to postpone your own assessment. Their participation can be helpful, but your recovery cannot depend on turning them into a co-clinician.

Action Challenge: Separate Support From Certainty

Make two short sentences you can use this week.

The first names a support request that does not require your partner to judge the thought: "Can you sit with me while I make the appointment?" "Can we agree that I will do bath time tonight even if I feel anxious?" "Can you take the baby for ten minutes while I reset, then hand her back so I do not turn the break into avoidance?"

The second names the certainty request you are trying not to outsource: "I notice I want you to tell me what this thought says about me. I am going to leave that question unanswered."

That difference is small enough to practice and large enough to change the shape of an evening.

Principles to Remember

Disclosure should have a purpose: honesty, practical planning, assessment, or support. It does not need to become confession for moral relief.

Family accommodation can reduce distress today while strengthening avoidance tomorrow. Partner involvement can be useful in treatment, but a partner should not become the therapist, risk assessor, or source of unlimited certainty.

Separate symptom conversations from workload conversations when possible. A mental-health explanation can increase compassion while the practical cost of avoidance still needs to change.

The healthiest disclosure is not the one that produces the strongest reassurance. It is the one that lets both people return to the relationship with clearer roles.

Chapter 8: When the Thought Is Sexual, Violent, or Taboo

The hardest intrusive thought is often not the loudest one. It is the one you cannot imagine saying out loud.

A new father may tell a clinician that he is "anxious around the baby" while leaving out the image that actually drives the fear. He may report poor sleep, irritability, or avoidance. He may say he hates bath time. What he does not say is that the feared thought feels sexual, violent, blasphemous, or morally repellent to him. He edits the sentence before anyone else can hear it.

That edit can keep a useful assessment from ever starting.

OCD is not limited to tidy, socially acceptable themes. Obsessions can attach themselves to what a person most wants certainty about, including harm, sexuality, morality, contamination, religion, relationships, and responsibility. Thought content can be shocking without functioning as intention. At the same time, no book can determine the meaning of a specific thought for a specific person. The clinical task is to assess the full pattern, including whether the thought is unwanted, how the person responds to it, whether there are compulsions or avoidance, and whether there are independent safety concerns. (Abramowitz et al., 2001; National Institute for Health and Care Excellence, 2005)

The principle of this chapter is simple: **the more shame a theme generates, the more important it is to describe the pattern accurately rather than letting shame make the diagnosis for you.**

This chapter will not print graphic examples. You do not need them to understand the mechanism, and another reader does not need a fresh set of images to carry.

Content Is Not the Whole Case

Suppose two people report a violent mental image.

One experiences it as unwanted, frightening, and inconsistent with what he wants. He spends hours checking his reactions, avoids holding the baby near certain objects, asks his partner whether he seems dangerous, and mentally reviews every moment of care.

The other reports desire, planning, or intent to act.

Those are not the same clinical presentation.

The words inside the thought are only one part of assessment. Form, context, appraisal, behavior, intent, and other symptoms matter. This is why self-diagnosis from a sentence on the internet is unreliable, and it is why a careful clinician asks questions that can initially feel uncomfortable.

Research and clinical literature on perinatal OCD has discussed intrusive thoughts of infant harm and the importance of distinguishing obsessional thoughts from conditions involving intent, psychosis, or other acute risk. Much of that literature is based on mothers, so it should not be lazily generalized as father-specific prevalence data. The underlying assessment distinction, however, is clinically important. (Hudak & Wisner, 2012)

A father who withholds the taboo content may accidentally make the pattern look vaguer than it is.

He may also lose months trying to solve the wrong problem.

The Shame Tax

Shame charges interest.

It makes you postpone the appointment. It makes you describe only half the symptom. It turns a search for help into a search for a perfect anonymous explanation. It can make you sit outside a therapist's office rehearsing a safer version of the truth.

Kenji did that.

His intake form asked what had brought him to treatment. He wrote, "Anxiety since baby was born."

Accurate, but not useful enough.

During the appointment he talked about work pressure, sleep loss, and feeling tense when alone with his son. Twenty-five minutes passed before the clinician asked what he feared might happen.

Kenji said, "I don't want to say it because then it will sound like I want it."

That sentence was more clinically useful than everything he had said before it.

The clinician did not answer by giving Kenji a moral certificate. She asked about whether the thoughts were wanted, what he did in response, how much he avoided, what he checked, whether there was intent or planning, and whether there were other symptoms that needed attention.

Kenji left without perfect certainty.

He also left with an assessment plan.

Those are different things.

Thought-Action Fusion Makes Taboo Content Sticky

Thought-action fusion is a term used in OCD research for beliefs that having a thought can make an event more likely or can be morally similar to performing an action. The concept has been studied as part of OCD-related cognition, although it is not exclusive to OCD. (Shafran & Rachman, 2004)

For a new father, the moral version can sound like this:

"If that appeared in my mind, there must be a reason."

"A good dad would never have that thought."

"If I can imagine it, I must be capable of it."

Notice what these statements do. They turn mental content into character evidence.

Then the checking begins.

Did I feel disgusted enough?

Did the thought arrive before or after I touched the baby?

Why did my body feel strange?

Would another father have had the same reaction?

The checking does not stay at the level of memory. It can spread into body monitoring. A person scans for sensations, then interprets the act of scanning as evidence that there was something to detect.

This is especially brutal with sexual intrusive thoughts because anxiety itself can make people monitor normal bodily sensations with extraordinary intensity. The aim of treatment is not to win a courtroom case about every sensation. It is to reduce the compulsive demand to use sensation as a verdict.

Action Challenge: Describe the Pattern, Not the Shock Value

If you are preparing for an OCD-informed assessment, write six plain facts.

When did the intrusive thought pattern begin?

Which caregiving situations trigger it?

What do you avoid because of it?

What do you check in your mind, body, memory, environment, or behavior?

What reassurance do you ask for?

How much time and participation is the loop taking from your day?

If there is intent, planning, a wish to act, loss of contact with reality, command experiences, severe agitation, intoxication, or any reason you are unsure whether someone is safe, say that directly and seek urgent in-person assessment. Do not use an OCD label to explain away a safety concern.

This exercise is not a diagnostic test. It is a way to give a clinician better information.

Do Not Use Disgust as a Home Test

Nikhil developed a private rule: if he felt enough disgust when the thought appeared, he was safe.

At first that sounded sensible to him.

Soon he was measuring disgust.

A thought appeared during a nappy change. Nikhil froze and checked his body. Was the disgust immediate? Strong enough? What if there had been a half-second of blankness first?

He replayed it during lunch.

Then he asked his partner whether a normal father would feel "instant horror."

The rule that was supposed to protect him had become another reassurance loop.

OCD is skilled at turning the evidence you collect into a new object of doubt.

If disgust is your proof, OCD will ask whether it was real.

If anxiety is your proof, it will ask whether the anxiety was strong enough.

If a therapist's sentence is your proof, it will ask whether you explained the thought accurately.

The goal is not to find an internal feeling that can certify you forever.

The goal is to stop requiring a certificate before you participate in ordinary care, while using appropriate clinical assessment for actual safety questions.

Why Detailed Confession Can Become a Compulsion

There is a difference between telling a clinician enough for assessment and telling your partner every version of a thought until you feel clean.

Confession can become a compulsion when its function is to obtain relief, forgiveness, or certainty again and again.

A father may say, "I need to be honest," when what he means is, "I need you to react in a way that makes the anxiety drop."

Five minutes later another detail appears.

"Actually, I should tell you one more thing."

Then another.

The partner becomes trapped in a role they never agreed to take.

This does not mean secrecy is the answer. It means the purpose of disclosure matters.

A clinician needs enough information to understand the pattern and assess risk. A partner may need enough information to understand why routines have changed and how to respond. Neither person necessarily needs a nightly transcript of every mental event.

That distinction protects honesty from being recruited by OCD.

The Body Is a Terrible Witness Stand

Taboo thoughts often pull attention toward the body.

Did my heart speed up?

Why did I feel numb?

Was that warmth?

Did I move automatically?

Body sensations are noisy. Anxiety, fatigue, posture, temperature, touch, movement, attention, and normal physiology can produce sensations that the mind then tries to interpret.

If you monitor closely enough, you will find something.

Then the certainty trap begins.

A father can spend an hour deciding whether a sensation was caused by fear, contact, embarrassment, adrenaline, or something else. The result is rarely confidence. It is usually more attention to the next sensation.

Response prevention in this context may involve allowing the uncertainty to remain without conducting the body investigation, when that approach has been planned appropriately with an OCD-informed clinician.

The aim is not indifference to safety.

It is refusing to make every body signal answer a moral question.

A Clinician Should Be Able to Hear the Theme

One reasonable test of a provider is whether you can describe the symptom without the room becoming a moral panic.

That does not mean a clinician should never ask direct safety questions. Good assessment may include very direct questions.

It means the clinician should know that unwanted intrusive thoughts, compulsions, avoidance, and thought-action fusion can occur in OCD, and should be able to distinguish assessment from reassurance.

If a provider appears unfamiliar with OCD or with exposure-based treatment, ask plainly:

"How do you assess intrusive harm thoughts in OCD?"

"Do you use CBT that includes exposure and response prevention?"

"How do you distinguish an obsession from intent or another condition?"

"How do you involve a partner without turning them into a reassurance source?"

NICE guidance recommends cognitive behavioral therapy that includes exposure and response prevention for OCD, with treatment intensity matched to impairment and preference. Medication options can also be considered clinically. (National Institute for Health and Care Excellence, 2005)

The right question is not whether a clinician promises never to feel concerned.

The right question is whether they can assess carefully without confusing taboo content with a conclusion.

When an Initial Reaction Hurts

Farid once disclosed a taboo thought to a professional who did not specialize in OCD.

The professional became visibly tense and asked a series of questions quickly. Some of those questions were appropriate safety questions. The speed and tone, however, convinced Farid that he had made a catastrophic mistake.

He stopped talking about the theme for months.

Later, an OCD specialist went through the same basic safety territory much more systematically. The difference was not that the specialist skipped risk. The difference was that the questions sat inside a coherent assessment of obsession, compulsion, avoidance, intent, and functioning.

If you have had a frightening disclosure experience, it can be tempting to conclude that silence is safer.

Silence may feel safer in the next ten minutes.

It can also prevent accurate care.

You are allowed to ask a provider about their experience with OCD. You are allowed to bring written notes. You are allowed to say, "I am afraid that saying this out loud will be misunderstood, so I need us to go carefully."

If you do not feel safe with the provider and there is no urgent risk requiring immediate action, seeking a clinician with stronger OCD expertise can be reasonable.

If there is urgent risk, do not delay urgent evaluation while searching for a perfect specialist.

Action Challenge: Write the First Two Sentences

Do not prepare a twenty-minute defense.

Prepare two sentences.

"I am having recurrent, unwanted intrusive thoughts about harm or taboo themes around my baby, and I have started avoiding care and checking myself because of them."

"I want an assessment that looks at OCD, compulsions, avoidance, and safety rather than asking me to decide what the thoughts mean on my own."

If another symptom is present, add it. If you have intent or planning, say it. If sleep, substance use, mania-like symptoms, hallucinations, or severe depression are part of the picture, include them.

Clarity beats a rehearsed innocence speech.

What You Are Practicing

The deepest practice in this chapter is not saying a forbidden word.

It is allowing a trained professional to assess you without first making yourself perfectly certain about the answer.

That is a reversal of the OCD arrangement.

OCD says: solve the moral question privately, then decide whether you are safe enough to ask for help.

A better sequence is: describe what is happening, receive an appropriate assessment, then work on the compulsions that keep demanding certainty.

The distinction matters because taboo content creates a special temptation to hide until you are sure.

But certainty is the thing the loop cannot reliably provide.

One more distinction is worth carrying forward. A thought can be both emotionally devastating and clinically ordinary within an obsessional pattern. Those statements are not opposites. Severity is not measured by how shocking a sentence sounds. It is measured by the whole pattern, the distress, the impairment, the compulsions, the avoidance, and any separate risk factors. That is why accurate assessment beats self-judgment.

In a Nutshell

Sexual, violent, and other taboo intrusive thoughts can occur in OCD, including around the transition to parenthood, but content alone does not determine diagnosis or risk. A careful assessment considers whether thoughts are unwanted, what the person does in response, the presence of compulsions and avoidance, intent, planning, reality testing, and other relevant symptoms.

Thought-action fusion can make a mental event feel like moral evidence. Body checking, disgust checking, memory review, reassurance, and repeated confession can then become attempts to settle the case.

Do not use this chapter to self-clear a safety concern. If there is intent, planning, a wish to act, loss of contact with reality, or uncertainty about immediate safety, seek urgent in-person help.

For obsessional patterns, the useful move is not a better private trial. It is accurate disclosure, appropriate assessment, and treatment that targets the response to the thought as well as the thought's content.

Chapter 9: When You Do Not Trust Yourself Alone With the Baby

The first solo hour can become a test you never agreed to take.

Your partner is putting on shoes. The baby is fed. The bag is packed. Nothing unusual is happening. Then your mind produces the sentence: *What if I lose control when nobody is here?*

You could ask your partner to stay.

You could call your mother and arrange for her to come over.

You could say you have a headache.

You could leave the baby in the cot and keep your distance until somebody returns.

Each option may lower your anxiety quickly. If the underlying pattern is OCD, however, the relief can teach your brain that being alone with your child was a situation that required escape.

The principle of this chapter is: **being alone with your child should not become a private safety exam, and re-entry works best when it is based on a clinical assessment and planned participation rather than repeated self-testing.**

This chapter assumes that a clinician has considered the safety picture when that is needed. It does not tell you to ignore intent, planning, psychosis, severe impairment, intoxication, or any reason you are unsure someone can provide safe care. In those situations, get appropriate in-person help and follow the safety plan you are given.

For an obsessional pattern, the problem is often different. The father is not trying to create an unsafe situation. He is trying to make ordinary care feel one hundred percent certified before he agrees to do it.

That certificate never arrives.

How Solo Care Becomes a Forbidden Zone

Owen had changed nappies and carried his son around the flat for weeks. He was tired, clumsy, and learning, but he was involved.

Then he had an intrusive image while holding the baby near the stairs.

The next day he asked his partner to carry the baby downstairs.

A few days later he stopped taking the baby upstairs alone.

Then he stopped being alone in the flat with him.

Owen explained each change as caution. He did not say, "I have built an avoidance system." He said, "There is no point taking chances."

The phrase was hard to argue with.

That is one reason avoidance can grow so far before anyone recognizes it. The language of safety is persuasive.

OCD-driven avoidance often has a hidden condition: *I will do this when I feel certain enough.*

Because the standard is certainty rather than reasonable safety, the condition keeps moving.

Reasonable Safety and the Certainty Trap

Every parent uses safety rules.

You use the correct car seat. You keep medications and dangerous objects out of reach. You follow safe-sleep guidance. You do not drive when dangerously impaired. You supervise a child in age-appropriate ways.

Those are ordinary risk-management behaviors.

The certainty trap asks for something else. It asks you to prove that you could never make a mistake, never have an impulse, never feel angry, never become distracted, and never experience another intrusive thought.

No parent can meet that standard.

The trick is that OCD dresses absolute certainty in the clothes of responsible parenting.

A useful question is not, "Can I prove nothing bad could ever happen?"

It is, "What would ordinary, evidence-based parenting require here if I were not using anxiety as the measuring instrument?"

That question does not erase risk. It returns risk to a human scale.

The Difference Between Support and a Safety Person

A partner can help you practice without becoming the condition that makes practice possible.

Darius wanted to resume solo bedtime. His first idea was to have his partner sit in the hallway.

That might be a reasonable early re-entry step in some treatment plans. The problem came when Darius decided she had to stay there until he felt calm.

Now her presence was not support. It was a safety signal.

The same thing can happen with video calls, open doors, constant texting, baby monitors used beyond their ordinary purpose, or a relative parked nearby "just in case."

The object is not automatically a compulsion.

Function matters.

If the monitor is being used as parents normally use it, that is different from staring at it to verify your own behavior every few seconds.

If your partner is home because that is the normal routine, that is different from requiring them to remain within hearing distance so you can feel cleared to change a nappy.

Treatment asks what the behavior is doing in the loop.

Action Challenge: Map the Conditions

Pick one caregiving task you currently avoid alone.

Write down every condition you believe must be true before you can do it.

"My partner must be in the house."

"I must not be tired."

"I must feel calm."

"I must not have had a bad thought that day."

"I must be able to call someone."

"I must keep the door open."

Now mark which conditions are ordinary childcare requirements and which are there mainly to reduce obsessional doubt.

Do not remove safety measures casually. Bring uncertain items to an OCD-informed clinician.

The point is to make the hidden rules visible.

Do Not Turn Solo Care Into Exposure Theater

Some fathers hear about exposure and immediately make it into another toughness test.

"Fine. I will prove I can do two hours alone."

That is not the spirit of the work.

Exposure is not a dare. It is a structured way of learning that anxiety and uncertainty can be present without compulsive escape or neutralizing. NICE recommends cognitive behavioral therapy including exposure and response prevention as a treatment approach for OCD, with the intensity matched to the person's level of impairment and circumstances. (National Institute for Health and Care Excellence, 2005)

A good re-entry step is large enough to matter and small enough that you can practice it repeatedly.

Ten minutes of solo floor play may be more useful than one heroic afternoon followed by a week of avoidance.

Repetition teaches more than spectacle.

The Stay-In Ladder Begins With What You Already Can Do

You will build the full Stay-In Ladder in the next chapter. For now, notice that re-entry does not have to begin at the top.

If you can feed the baby while your partner showers, that is a foothold.

If you can carry the baby from the bedroom to the kitchen but avoid the stairs, that is information.

If you can do nappies except when a particular intrusive theme is loud, that identifies a trigger.

If you can be alone for five minutes but not thirty, that gives you a starting point.

OCD tends to describe the situation globally: "I cannot be alone with the baby."

The actual pattern is usually more specific.

Specificity creates options.

What to Do When Anxiety Spikes Mid-Care

Jamal had been alone with his daughter for twelve minutes when his anxiety jumped.

His old sequence was immediate: place the baby somewhere safe, text his partner, search a forum, and wait for the feeling to pass before resuming contact.

His treatment plan changed the sequence.

He still used ordinary childcare safety. He placed the baby appropriately when he needed both hands. But he did not use distance as a moral cleansing ritual.

He named what was happening: "Intrusive thought, anxiety, reassurance urge."

He allowed the feeling to be present without solving the thought.

Then he returned attention to the next caregiving action: bottle, burp cloth, nappy, floor time.

The skill was not becoming calm on command.

The skill was continuing with the task while calm was unavailable.

That distinction matters because "I must calm down before I care for my child" can become another hidden condition.

Anger Does Not Automatically Mean the Same Thing as an Obsession

Solo care can be stressful even without OCD.

A crying baby, severe sleep loss, relationship conflict, depression, substance use, or a history of anger problems can change what support is needed.

Do not force every difficult feeling into the OCD explanation.

Research on paternal postpartum depression has described anger and frustration among some fathers, but that evidence is not proof that anger is a defining feature of paternal harm OCD. (Pedersen et al., 2021)

If you are worried about what you do when angry, tell a clinician the behavioral facts.

Have you shouted?

Have you thrown or broken things?

Have you felt close to acting in a way that scares you?

Do you use substances when caring for the baby?

Do you lose time or contact with reality?

Those facts matter more than an internet category.

If you believe your child or anyone else may be in immediate danger, stop using a book as the decision-maker. Arrange safe care and seek urgent professional help.

The Monitor Problem

Technology can make a reassurance loop look modern.

Ben installed a camera because the baby was moving into a separate room. Ordinary decision.

Within a week he was reviewing clips of himself carrying the baby.

He checked whether his hands looked "normal."

He replayed moments after intrusive thoughts.

He zoomed in on facial expressions.

The camera had become a witness in the trial.

Deleting the camera might not solve the problem. He could simply move the checking into memory.

In treatment, Ben kept the monitor for its ordinary purpose and stopped using recorded footage to inspect himself.

The aim was not technological purity.

It was response prevention.

Ask: "Would I use this device this way if I were not trying to settle the obsession?"

That question can reveal a compulsion hiding inside a normal parenting tool.

Reassurance Before Handover

Another common ritual happens at the door.

"You're sure you're okay leaving me?"

"You think I seem normal?"

"What if I get overwhelmed?"

"Do you trust me?"

The partner answers.

The father feels relief.

Then the partner reaches for the handle and the doubt returns.

One more question.

This can make every handover feel like an airport security check.

A different handover is shorter.

"The plan is one hour. I know what the baby's routine is. If there is a real childcare problem, I will contact you the way we agreed. I am not going to use you to answer the OCD question."

That is not a magic script.

It is a change in function.

You are planning care rather than asking for a character verdict.

Action Challenge: Run a Short Re-Entry

Choose a re-entry step that is appropriate for your situation and, if you are in treatment, consistent with your plan.

Set the task by behavior, not by feeling.

"I will do ten minutes of floor play while my partner is in another room."

Not: "I will do floor play until I feel safe."

During the task, notice reassurance urges, checking, mental review, and escape plans.

Do not grade yourself on anxiety.

Grade only whether you practiced the chosen response.

Afterward, do not conduct a postmortem.

Write one sentence: "I did the step, anxiety was present at ___ out of ten, and I practiced not doing ___."

Then move on with the day.

The post-exposure analysis can become a compulsion as easily as the pre-exposure debate.

What Your Partner May Need From You

When you have avoided solo care for weeks or months, re-entry is not only about your symptoms.

Your partner may be exhausted.

They may be angry.

They may have stopped trusting promises because tasks were repeatedly handed back.

Do not ask them to celebrate every exposure while also carrying the workload created by the avoidance.

Recovery includes repair.

That might mean taking on a predictable shift, not just doing a symbolic ten-minute task.

It might mean acknowledging, "My avoidance has left you with more care. I am working on the OCD pattern, and I also need to rebuild reliability."

A diagnosis can explain a pattern without erasing its impact.

That is adult partnership.

If You Live Separately From Your Child

Not every father shares a home with his child.

You may be co-parenting after separation. You may have scheduled contact. You may be a non-gestational parent in a family with complicated logistics. You may be dealing with legal arrangements that this book cannot interpret for you.

The principle still applies: do not let OCD quietly write the parenting schedule.

If you are avoiding contact because of intrusive thoughts, disclose that to an appropriate clinician.

If there are legal orders or child-protection requirements, follow them and get qualified legal advice where needed. Do not use a general mental-health book to override formal arrangements.

Re-entry may need coordination with treatment, the other parent, and any relevant professionals.

The goal remains involvement that is both clinically appropriate and practically responsible.

When the Baby Is No Longer a Baby

By the second year, the feared situations change.

A toddler climbs.

They reach for objects.

They protest.

They run toward the least convenient danger in the room.

A father's avoidance can therefore change shape. It may move from nappies and bath time to playgrounds, stairs, kitchen tasks, carrying a protesting toddler, or being responsible during a tantrum.

The central issue is not the exact task.

It is whether obsessional doubt is deciding how much fatherhood you are allowed to do.

The Stay-In Ladder is designed to move with those changes.

It is not a baby-only tool.

The Point of Being There

A child does not receive your internal certainty score. They receive your behavior: the bottle you prepare, the book you read, the nappy you change, the hand you offer, the limit you set, the ordinary return after a hard moment.

That is useful because behavior is trainable even when thoughts are noisy. It gives you something concrete to build deliberately.

Principles to Remember

Solo care should not become a private exam in which you must prove perfect safety before you participate. Ordinary parenting uses reasonable safety practices. OCD adds a demand for certainty that no parent can satisfy.

For an obsessional pattern, avoidance and safety signals can keep the feared situation feeling exceptional. Re-entry is better built through repeatable, appropriately planned steps than through heroic tests.

Do not collapse every concern into OCD. Anger, depression, substance use, psychosis, severe sleep deprivation, intent, planning, and other risk factors need their own assessment. If immediate safety is uncertain, seek urgent in-person help.

When the clinical picture is consistent with OCD, measure practice by participation and reduced compulsive responding, not by how calm you feel.

The aim is not to become a father who never has a frightening thought.

It is to stop requiring the thought to disappear before you do the next ordinary piece of care.

PART III: GETTING BACK IN

A practical return to ordinary fatherhood.

Chapter 10: The Stay-In Ladder

Exposure and response prevention is a clinical treatment method. The Stay-In Ladder is not a replacement for it.

It is a fatherhood-facing way to organize one practical problem that shows up again and again in these pages: how do you re-enter the pieces of care that fear has made you avoid, while reducing the rituals that keep those situations feeling dangerous?

The ladder has three jobs.

First, it turns the global sentence "I cannot trust myself around my child" into specific situations you can describe.

Second, it separates the caregiving action from the compulsion you have been using to get through it.

Third, it gives you a way to practice staying involved without making comfort the price of admission.

The principle is: **build participation in steps, and measure the step by what you did rather than by whether your mind finally agreed that you were safe.**

For anyone with unresolved safety concerns, intent, planning, psychotic symptoms, severe impairment, intoxication, or uncertainty about safe childcare, assessment comes before self-directed exposure. The ladder assumes that ordinary participation is clinically appropriate.

Step One: Name the Life You Are Trying to Get Back

A ladder without a destination becomes another OCD project.

Do not begin by ranking fears.

Begin by naming the fathering behavior that matters.

"I want to do bedtime twice a week."

"I want to take my daughter to the playground alone."

"I want to change nappies without calling my partner into the room."

"I want to cook while my toddler plays nearby."

"I want to carry my son downstairs without rehearsing disaster."

This is values-led parenting in a concrete form. The value is not a slogan like "be present." The value has a calendar.

Tomas wrote, "Saturday breakfast with my son while my wife sleeps."

That sentence gave his treatment work a reason.

He was not exposing himself to discomfort because discomfort was noble. He was making room for a piece of fatherhood that had been missing.

Step Two: Break the Goal Into Observable Re-Entry Steps

Global goals invite global fear.

Specific actions give you something to practice.

Suppose the goal is solo bath time.

A sequence might begin with preparing the towel and clothes while your partner does the bath. Then you might do the washing while your partner is in the room but occupied with something else. Next, you might do the full bath while your partner is elsewhere in the home. Later, if clinically appropriate and consistent with ordinary childcare needs, you might do the routine while you are the only adult home.

That is only an illustration.

Your steps should fit your actual family, your child's age, ordinary safety practices, and your treatment plan.

The important feature is that each step is a behavior you can recognize.

"Feel less anxious" is not a step.

"Change one nappy without asking my partner to observe me" is.

Step Three: Name the Compulsion Attached to Each Step

This is the part fathers often miss.

They create a ladder of feared situations but carry every ritual up the ladder with them.

Luis resumed bath time but mentally reviewed every hand movement afterward.

Kenji resumed nappies but required the bathroom door to remain open.

Owen resumed solo care but texted his partner every five minutes.

Darius resumed bedtime but monitored his body for "wrong" sensations.

The caregiving behavior returned. The OCD rules remained.

For each re-entry step, ask: What do I usually do to make this feel safe enough?

That may be reassurance, checking, mental review, confession, body monitoring, internet searching, avoidance of particular objects, repeated prayer used as neutralization, or arranging another adult as a safety signal.

Then decide which response you are practicing not doing.

This is why the second half of ERP matters. Exposure without response prevention can become exposure plus ritual.

NICE guidance describes CBT including ERP as a treatment for OCD and recommends matching the level of intervention to impairment and patient preference. (National Institute for Health and Care Excellence, 2005)

Step Four: Make the Step Repeatable

The best ladder step is not the one that impresses you.

It is the one you can repeat.

Gabriel initially chose a dramatic target: a whole Saturday alone with the baby.

His clinician asked how often he could practice that.

Once every few weeks.

They chose a smaller step instead: the first forty-five minutes after work, three evenings each week.

That was less cinematic.

It was more useful.

Repeated learning gives your brain more chances to discover that anxiety can rise and fall without the old response.

It also rebuilds family reliability. Your partner can plan around a repeated shift more easily than around occasional heroic acts.

Action Challenge: Build the First Four Rungs

Write one concrete fathering goal.

Under it, write four re-entry steps from easier to harder.

For each step, add one line that begins, "The compulsion I will practice reducing is..."

Then add frequency.

"Three times this week."

"Every Tuesday and Thursday."

"Once each weekend for the next month."

If you are working with a clinician, bring the ladder to treatment. Let them help you adjust steps that are too small to teach anything, too large to repeat, or mixed with actual safety questions.

The Stay-In Ladder is a planning surface, not a diagnosis.

Do Not Rank by Fear Alone

Traditional exposure hierarchies often use subjective distress ratings. Those can be useful.

For fathers, I want you to add another dimension: family value.

A task can be moderately scary and extremely important.

Another can be extremely scary but barely relevant to your life.

If you organize the entire plan around fear intensity, OCD still gets to set the agenda.

Consider two tasks.

One father is highly anxious about carrying the baby past a particular kitchen drawer, but there is no practical reason he needs to do that route often.

He is moderately anxious about doing the bedtime bottle, which his partner currently handles every night because he avoids it.

The bedtime bottle may deserve earlier attention because it returns something meaningful to the family.

Your ladder is not a museum of fears.

It is a route back into your life.

The Three Scores

For each rung, you can track three simple scores before planning the next one.

Participation: Did I do the caregiving action I chose?

Compulsion: Did I reduce the ritual I had targeted?

Value: Did this step return something that matters to my role as a father or partner?

Do not add a fourth score called "Did I feel safe?"

That question will try to take over the sheet.

Anxiety ratings can be clinically useful, especially in treatment, but the fatherhood scorecard here deliberately emphasizes behavior.

If your anxiety was eight out of ten and you did the planned behavior without the reassurance ritual, that may be a strong practice.

If your anxiety was two and you performed the ritual for twenty minutes afterward, the calm feeling does not make the practice more useful.

What Counts as Staying In

Staying in does not mean physically gripping a situation until you are overwhelmed.

It means remaining engaged with the chosen caregiving action while dropping the unnecessary escape or neutralizing response you and your clinician have identified.

Sometimes that involves completing the task.

Sometimes it involves returning after a brief, ordinary pause.

Sometimes it means allowing your partner to help because two adults normally share the task, while not using their presence as proof that you are morally safe.

Context matters.

A rigid rule such as "I can never step away" would be another bad certainty rule.

Parents sometimes need breaks. Babies sometimes need to be placed in a safe location while an adult resets. Partners take turns. Those are normal.

The question is whether the break serves ordinary regulation and childcare, or whether it is becoming a ritualized escape from obsessional doubt.

When the Step Goes Badly

Nikhil's first planned solo nappy change went badly by his standards.

The baby was crying.

A taboo intrusive thought arrived.

Nikhil froze.

He checked his body for a few seconds before remembering the plan.

Then he finished the nappy change.

Afterward he asked his partner, "Do you think I handled that normally?"

Halfway through the sentence, he realized he had reached for reassurance.

His first conclusion was, "I failed the exposure."

That conclusion was too crude.

He had practiced a new behavior, slipped into two old responses, noticed them, and had data for the next attempt.

Treatment is not a purity test.

If you turn every rung into pass or fail, perfectionism joins the OCD team.

The useful review is brief: What did I do? Which compulsion showed up? What will I practice next time?

Then stop reviewing.

Response Prevention After the Task

The ten minutes after caregiving can matter as much as the task itself.

Many fathers can get through the bath, nappy, bottle, or walk. Then the mental court opens.

Did I stand too close?

Why did that thought come then?

Was I irritated?

Did I enjoy the wrong part?

What if I missed something?

Post-task review can become a delayed compulsion.

So every Stay-In rung needs an after-plan.

For five or ten minutes after the task, return to ordinary life.

Wash the bottle.

Put away the towel.

Answer an email.

Read with your child.

Talk to your partner about something unrelated.

You are not distracting yourself to make the thought vanish. You are declining to give the thought a scheduled hearing.

Action Challenge: Create an After-Plan

For one rung, write the first ordinary action you will take after completing it.

Then write the ritual you expect to feel pulled toward.

"After bath time, I will put the clothes in the laundry. I expect an urge to replay how I held him."

"After the playground, I will make lunch. I expect an urge to search whether other dads have thoughts like mine."

"After the nappy, I will continue the morning routine. I expect an urge to confess the exact thought."

A planned exit from the task can prevent the OCD debrief from swallowing the win.

When Your Partner Wants the Ladder Faster

Recovery affects another adult's workload.

That creates tension.

Your partner may look at a four-week plan and think, *I have already been doing all of this for four months.*

Their frustration can be valid.

Your need for graded work can also be valid.

Do not solve this by pretending one of those facts is false.

Have two conversations.

The treatment conversation asks, "What progression gives me the best chance of reducing avoidance and compulsions?"

The household conversation asks, "How do we distribute the remaining work fairly while I am rebuilding these tasks?"

Sometimes the answer includes you taking on other duties immediately while the feared caregiving tasks return gradually.

Treatment should not become a permanent exemption from adult contribution.

When You Want the Ladder Slower

OCD will always offer a reason to postpone the next rung.

This week was stressful.

The thought was worse yesterday.

The baby is teething.

You did not sleep well.

Your partner seems nervous.

Some of those conditions matter. Others are the certainty trap wearing a practical hat.

Set progression rules with your clinician before the anxiety spike if you can.

For example: "After I repeat this rung three times while practicing the planned response prevention, I will discuss moving up."

That protects the plan from being renegotiated by every bad morning.

Drop One Safety Signal at a Time

A father may have built a dense web of safety signals.

Partner in the room.

Phone unlocked.

Door open.

Certain objects moved.

Baby monitor recording.

Specific route through the house.

A phrase repeated silently.

Removing all of them at once can make practice unnecessarily chaotic.

A clinician may help you choose which response to reduce first.

The goal is not maximal discomfort.

The goal is learning that can be repeated in ordinary family life, not endurance for its own sake.

That distinction is important because macho exposure can be as unhelpful as avoidance. You do not need to prove courage by making a task harsher than ordinary fatherhood requires.

You are training flexibility, reliability, and a different response to uncertainty.

The Ladder Has a Top, but Life Keeps Moving

When you reach a goal, do not retire the skill.

Children change.

The six-month-old who lay on a mat becomes the fourteen-month-old who opens cupboards.

The toddler who loved the bath begins resisting it.

Travel, illness, nursery, family visits, and sleep changes create new situations.

The Stay-In Ladder is reusable because the method stays the same.

Name the fathering behavior.

Break it into observable re-entry steps.

Name the compulsive response.

Practice reducing that response.

Repeat.

Move toward the life that matters, not toward a feeling of permanent certainty.

A Note on Setbacks

Aaron completed months of solo care and then had a severe spike after a stressful week.

His first reaction was, "I am back at the beginning."

He was not.

The intrusive thoughts felt familiar, but Aaron now recognized the reassurance loop within minutes.

He shortened a couple of tasks temporarily after discussing the spike in treatment, then resumed the plan.

The old fear had returned.

The old ignorance had not.

That difference matters.

Recovery does not mean never revisiting a rung. It means you know what the ladder is for.

Action Challenge: Write the Maintenance Rule

Finish this sentence:

"If an old fear returns, I will treat it as a signal to practice the method again, not as proof that the method failed."

Then add one person you can contact if you start rebuilding a large avoidance system.

That might be your therapist, prescriber, primary-care clinician, partner, or another appropriate support.

The earlier you notice the retreat, the fewer rungs you may need to rebuild.

Principles to Remember

The Stay-In Ladder translates a frightening global belief into specific fathering actions. It is built around participation, response prevention, repetition, and value.

A useful rung names both the caregiving task and the compulsion you are reducing. Re-entering the task while keeping every ritual intact can leave the OCD rule untouched.

Practice should be repeatable rather than heroic. Add family value to fear ratings so the plan moves toward the fatherhood you actually want, not merely toward whichever fear looks most impressive on paper.

Plan for the minutes after the task, when mental review and reassurance can arrive late.

A setback does not erase prior learning. Children change and fear themes change. The ladder is a practical method you can reuse as family life changes.

When safety is genuinely uncertain, assessment comes first. When the pattern is obsessional and ordinary care is appropriate, the goal is not to feel perfectly certain on each rung.

The goal is to keep building a fatherhood that is larger than the loop, one repeatable step at a time.

Chapter 11: Nappies, Bath Time, Stairs, Kitchens, and Other Ordinary Care

A nappy is not a psychological test.

Neither is a bath.

Neither is carrying a baby down the stairs, standing at a kitchen counter while your toddler plays nearby, fastening a car seat, giving a bottle, changing clothes, reading a book, or holding a child who is upset.

OCD can turn any of these ordinary actions into a courtroom.

The task begins. The intrusive thought arrives. Attention leaves the child and swings inward. You monitor your hands, your feelings, your body, your memory, your tone of voice. You complete the task, then review it.

The result is strange: you can be physically present and psychologically absent at the same time.

The principle of this chapter is: **ordinary care becomes easier to reclaim when you return attention to the job in front of you and stop treating each task as evidence about the kind of father you are.**

This is not a chapter of childcare instructions. Use reliable pediatric and public-health guidance for practical safety. It is a chapter about the OCD rules that can attach themselves to routine care.

Nappies: When Intimacy Becomes Evidence

Nappy changes can become a major trigger for fathers with sexual or harm-related intrusive thoughts.

The practical task is simple and intimate. That combination gives OCD plenty to work with.

A father may begin avoiding changes when his partner is available.

Then he may require the door open.

Then he may rush.

Then he may check his body.

Then he may mentally replay whether his touch was appropriate.

The changing mat becomes less about the child and more about monitoring the father.

Hugo described the shift in one sentence: "I was doing every nappy with a camera pointed inward."

His response-prevention work was not to become careless.

It was to do the ordinary care appropriately without using body sensations, disgust, anxiety, speed, or post-task memory review as moral evidence.

The child needed a clean nappy.

That was the job.

The Ordinary-Task Question

Before a routine care task, ask:

"What does this task require in ordinary parenting terms?"

That question directs attention outward.

A nappy change requires the practical steps of changing the child safely and appropriately.

A bath requires age-appropriate supervision and water safety.

Stairs require ordinary care in carrying or accompanying a child.

Cooking requires keeping a child away from hazards and following normal kitchen safety.

The certainty trap adds invisible tasks:

Monitor your mind.

Prove your intentions.

Check your body.

Never feel irritated.

Never have a strange sensation.

Never have an intrusive image.

Remember every second accurately.

Those extra jobs are impossible to finish.

Action Challenge: Find the Invisible Job

Choose one routine you dread.

Write the ordinary parenting job in one sentence.

Then write the invisible OCD job underneath it.

"Ordinary job: change my son's nappy safely and get him dressed."

"Invisible job: prove I did not think, feel, or touch anything that could mean something bad."

The second job is where the loop lives.

If you are working with a clinician, show them the pair. It can help you identify response prevention that leaves normal safety intact.

Bath Time: The Task That Became a Symbol

Aaron stopped doing bath time after one intrusive thought.

Months later, bath time no longer felt like a task. It felt like the place where the thought had happened.

That symbolic weight made re-entry harder.

His first return was awkward. He noticed every movement. He watched his anxiety. He could hear the thought asking whether he felt "normal enough."

Then his son slapped the water and soaked Aaron's shirt.

For several seconds Aaron was just annoyed about being wet.

That moment mattered.

Not because distraction cured OCD.

Because the task had become a task again.

Bath time had water, toys, shampoo, towels, an impatient child, and a floor that needed drying. It contained more than the obsession.

Exposure can restore dimensionality to situations that OCD has flattened into one feared meaning.

Stairs: Responsibility Without Omnipotence

Stairs can trigger accidental-harm obsessions.

The father imagines a fall.

Then he starts treating the image as a forecast.

Reasonable safety matters. Carry children in ways appropriate to their age and your physical ability. Keep the environment safe. Do not carry a child when you are impaired.

But ordinary safety does not include a guarantee against every conceivable accident.

Responsibility is not omnipotence.

That distinction is central to harm OCD.

You can be responsible for using reasonable care without being responsible for eliminating all uncertainty from physical life.

The demand to eliminate uncertainty is not a higher form of love.

It is an impossible contract.

The Grip Check

Luis noticed that he squeezed his daughter harder on the stairs whenever an intrusive image appeared.

He believed the extra grip proved he was being careful.

Then he began checking whether the grip was strong enough.

He went up and down slowly.

He avoided carrying anything else.

He asked his partner to watch.

The safety behavior was multiplying.

His clinician helped him distinguish ordinary carrying from anxiety-driven overcontrol.

The lesson was uncomfortable: sometimes an attempt to feel safer can make the body stiffer, attention narrower, and the task more awkward.

The goal was not to carry casually.

It was to carry normally.

That word, normally, is not a perfect standard. It means according to ordinary childcare and situational safety rather than according to an obsessional need for certainty.

Kitchens: When Objects Acquire Meaning

A kitchen contains sharp, hot, heavy, breakable, electrical, and messy things.

It is therefore a rich setting for harm OCD.

Some fathers begin removing ordinary objects far beyond age-appropriate childproofing.

They put knives in another room even when the child cannot access them.

They refuse to cook while alone with the baby.

They ask their partner to enter the kitchen first.

They position themselves according to an elaborate private geometry.

The key question is not whether kitchens contain hazards. They do.

The question is whether your precautions are proportionate to ordinary family safety or designed mainly to neutralize an intrusive thought about your own intent.

That distinction can be hard to make from inside the loop. Bring it to treatment.

Action Challenge: The Ordinary-Safety Audit

Pick one room where your rules have expanded.

List the safety measures that are based on ordinary childcare guidance.

Then list the measures that appeared after intrusive thoughts and are aimed at preventing *you* from becoming the danger.

Do not remove anything you are unsure about on the strength of this exercise alone.

The purpose is to identify questions for an OCD-informed clinician.

OCD thrives when every private rule remains unnamed.

Car Seats, Driving, and Responsibility

Driving can combine several OCD themes at once.

Harm.

Responsibility.

Checking.

Memory.

"What if I did not fasten the buckle correctly?"

"What if I lose control while driving?"

"What if I hit something and did not notice?"

A father may check the buckle repeatedly.

He may photograph it.

He may drive only when another adult is present.

He may retrace routes.

There is an ordinary safety action here: fit and use the car seat correctly according to manufacturer and safety guidance.

The compulsion begins when checking no longer serves a reasonable practical purpose and instead seeks a feeling of certainty that lasts only until the next doubt.

One correct check can be safety.

Seven checks may be ritual.

The exact number is not universal. Function and context matter.

The One-Check Problem

OCD loves numerical rules because they feel objective.

"Only check once."

That can be useful in a treatment plan.

It can also become a new ritual if the father begins obsessing over whether the one check was done perfectly.

The deeper skill is tolerating the remaining uncertainty after reasonable action.

That may mean you fasten the car seat according to normal procedure, perform the ordinary check you have agreed on, and leave without reopening the buckle three times.

The goal is not worshipping the number one.

It is ending the search for an impossible final feeling.

Crying: When Irritation Becomes a Character Test

Babies cry.

Toddlers scream.

Parents become irritated.

For a father with harm obsessions, ordinary irritation can feel incriminating.

The sequence can be immediate.

The baby will not settle.

The father feels anger.

An intrusive image appears.

He concludes that the anger caused or revealed the image.

Now he checks whether he is too angry to be safe.

This requires nuance.

Irritation is not proof of intent.

It also does not mean every behavior while angry is harmless.

If you are frightened by your behavior, feel close to losing control, have acted aggressively, or are unsure you can provide safe care, place the child in an appropriate safe situation, arrange support, and seek professional assessment. Follow pediatric guidance about coping with crying and never shake a baby.

For obsessional doubt without intent, repeatedly treating the feeling of irritation as a risk test can become another checking loop.

The clinical picture matters more than the emotion's existence.

Reset Without Retreat

A reset can be ordinary parenting.

You place the baby safely in the cot and step into the next room for a brief moment because the crying has overwhelmed you.

You breathe.

You get water.

You return.

That can be sensible regulation.

The same physical action can function differently if it becomes, "I must leave every time an intrusive thought appears because my presence is dangerous."

The behavior does not tell you its function.

The rule around it does.

A useful plan separates a normal reset from an OCD retreat.

For example: "If I am overloaded by crying, I will use the safe-break plan we agreed on. I will not automatically abandon the rest of the caregiving shift because an intrusive thought occurred."

If you need help deciding what is appropriate, use a clinician and reliable parenting guidance.

Play: The Avoidance Nobody Notices

Not all retreat looks serious.

A father may avoid rough-and-tumble play because an intrusive thought once appeared.

He may avoid lying on the floor.

He may stop tickling.

He may keep physical affection stiff and brief.

Because the child is still fed and clean, nobody labels this avoidance.

But play is part of a relationship.

So is spontaneous affection.

OCD can shrink those domains quietly.

Kenji noticed he was always the photographer.

At the park he stood three meters away and took pictures while his partner climbed, pushed the swing, and chased their son.

Photography was not the problem.

The distance was.

His Stay-In Ladder eventually included "phone in pocket, ten minutes on the floor."

That was not an exposure to a random fear.

It was a return to play.

Bedtime: The Nightly Reassurance Window

Bedtime often combines fatigue and quiet, two conditions in which intrusive thoughts can feel louder.

A father may complete the routine, then stare at the baby monitor.

He may return to the room repeatedly.

He may review the day.

He may ask his partner, "Do you think I seemed off tonight?"

The hour after the child sleeps can become the OCD shift.

This is where an after-plan helps.

Finish the ordinary safety routine.

Then deliberately return to adult life.

Shower.

Read.

Prepare lunch.

Talk about something other than symptoms.

Watch something silly.

Go to sleep when you can.

Do not use the quiet as an invitation to prosecute the day.

Action Challenge: Reclaim One Ordinary Detail

Choose a routine you are already doing but doing under heavy self-monitoring.

Do not make the task harder.

Choose one small piece of attention to return to the child or the environment.

At bath time, listen to the child's sounds rather than your mental commentary.

During a bottle, notice the sequence of the routine rather than scanning your body.

At the park, keep the phone away for five minutes and join the play.

During bedtime, read the actual page rather than the thought.

This is not mindfulness used as a trick to make anxiety disappear.

It is attention serving the task you chose.

If the thought stays, the task can still continue.

What Happens When the Child Resists

Toddlerhood introduces negotiation.

The child refuses the nappy.

They arch in the car seat.

They hit.

They bite.

They run.

A father with harm OCD may become terrified of using ordinary physical guidance because any firm contact feels morally loaded.

He may also become afraid of his irritation.

This is another area where OCD treatment and parenting guidance need to remain distinct.

Learn age-appropriate parenting strategies from trustworthy sources.

Use the least force necessary for ordinary safety and care.

If you are unsure what is appropriate, ask a pediatric professional or parenting specialist.

Do not invent your own parenting standard from the intensity of an intrusive thought.

OCD is not a child-development expert.

When Your Child Notices

Older toddlers notice routines.

They may ask why Dad never does the bath.

They may reach for the other parent.

They may protest when you re-enter a task they associate with someone else.

Do not turn the child's reaction into evidence.

A toddler preferring the usual bedtime parent is a toddler preferring a routine, not a verdict on your recovery.

Keep explanations age-appropriate and simple.

You do not need to disclose adult obsessional content to a young child.

"Dad is doing bath tonight."

"We both take care of you."

"You're used to Mum doing this. Tonight it's my turn."

The aim is to make your return ordinary.

Reliability Is More Important Than Drama

A family rarely needs one giant act of courage.

It needs Tuesday night bath.

Saturday breakfast.

The nursery pickup.

The nappy nobody wants to change.

The toddler who asks for the same book again.

Recovery becomes visible through repetition.

This is one reason values-led parenting matters. It turns symptom work into a schedule of actual contribution.

Your child does not need a father who wins a private argument with every thought.

Your family needs a father who can keep returning to ordinary care with appropriate safety, flexibility, and help when help is needed.

In a Nutshell

OCD can turn routine care into evidence-gathering. Nappies, baths, stairs, kitchens, car seats, crying, play, and bedtime become places where a father monitors his thoughts, body, memory, or character.

Separate the ordinary parenting job from the invisible certainty job.

Use reliable childcare guidance for practical safety. Use OCD-informed treatment for the compulsions and avoidance that have attached themselves to those tasks. Do not ask a mental-health exercise to replace pediatric, legal, or safety advice.

Reasonable care is not the same as eliminating all possible risk.

A brief break can be normal regulation or OCD-driven retreat depending on its function. A single check can be practical or ritualized depending on what it is trying to settle.

Reclaim ordinary details. Rebuild repeatable tasks. Let care become care again.

The target is not a perfect internal state.

It is reliable participation in the ordinary work and ordinary pleasure of raising your child.

Chapter 12: Get Help That Understands OCD

A treatment recommendation is only useful if you can get through the door, describe what is happening, and recognize whether the help on offer actually fits the problem.

For fathers, that first part can be harder than it sounds.

Research on paternal mental health has repeatedly described barriers such as low recognition of symptoms, stigma, masculine norms, practical access problems, and services that fathers may experience as oriented primarily toward mothers. A 2024 study of fathers' help-seeking around perinatal mental health likewise reported barriers involving awareness, stigma, and the way services are organized. (Reay et al., 2024)

That evidence is broader than OCD. It should not be used to claim that every father with harm obsessions will avoid care for the same reason. It does help explain why "just find a therapist" is not an adequate instruction.

The principle of this chapter is: **look for a provider who can assess the whole picture and who understands OCD treatment well enough to target compulsions and avoidance, not just help you feel better about the content of the thought.**

You do not need to become an expert in diagnostic criteria before making the call. You do need a few practical questions.

Start With the Problem, Not the Label

You may be fairly sure this is OCD.

You may not be sure at all.

Either way, describe the pattern.

"I began having recurrent, unwanted intrusive thoughts after the baby arrived."

"I avoid being alone with my child."

"I ask my partner for reassurance several times a day."

"I replay caregiving moments in my head."

"I check my body and reactions."

"I am frightened of what the thoughts might mean."

That description gives a clinician material to assess.

Saying only "I have harm OCD" can sometimes shortcut useful questions.

Saying only "I am stressed" can hide the most important pattern.

Bring both the content and the behavior.

What an OCD-Informed Assessment Should Notice

A careful assessment is broader than counting intrusive thoughts.

The clinician may ask about when the thoughts started, whether they are unwanted, the situations that trigger them, what you do to neutralize them, how much you avoid, how much time the loop consumes, and how it affects work, sleep, relationships, and parenting.

They may also ask about mood, substance use, psychotic symptoms, trauma, anger, medications, medical factors, sleep, intent, planning, and other safety issues.

Those questions are not evidence that the clinician has decided you are dangerous.

They are part of making sure the OCD explanation is not being used to cover a different or additional problem.

A good assessment can hold two ideas at once: taboo intrusive thoughts can occur in OCD, and risk still deserves proper assessment when there are relevant signs.

The Treatment Phrase to Know

The phrase you should recognize is **cognitive behavioral therapy with exposure and response prevention**, often shortened to CBT with ERP.

NICE guidance for OCD recommends CBT including ERP, with different levels of treatment depending on severity and impairment. It also discusses selective serotonin reuptake inhibitors as a medication option in appropriate cases. (National Institute for Health and Care Excellence, 2005)

This book cannot tell you which treatment intensity or medication is right for you.

It can help you ask whether a provider understands the treatment model.

"What experience do you have treating OCD?"

"Do you use exposure and response prevention?"

"How do you work with mental compulsions and reassurance, not just visible rituals?"

"How do you assess taboo intrusive thoughts and distinguish them from intent or other conditions?"

"How would you involve my partner if family accommodation is part of the loop?"

You are not interviewing for perfection.

You are checking fit.

Why Reassurance-Only Therapy Can Stall

A caring therapist may hear a frightened father and respond, "You would never do that. You love your baby."

The father feels better.

For an hour.

Then the mind asks whether the therapist understood every detail.

The father returns with another variation.

The therapist reassures again.

A therapeutic relationship can accidentally become a higher-status reassurance loop.

This does not mean compassion is harmful.

It means compassion should not be confused with repeated certainty-giving when certainty-seeking is part of the problem.

ERP-oriented treatment usually asks the person to face obsessional triggers while reducing the compulsive responses used to neutralize anxiety. The exact exercises should be individualized and should not ignore real-world safety.

When a Provider Does Not Know Perinatal OCD

You may find an excellent OCD therapist who has little experience with new fathers.

You may find a perinatal mental-health clinician who understands the transition to parenthood but has less training in ERP.

Neither fact automatically disqualifies them.

Ask what they know and how they would fill the gap.

A provider who understands OCD well can often learn the fatherhood context.

A perinatal provider can consult or refer for OCD-specific treatment.

What matters is whether somebody in the care plan understands the obsession-compulsion cycle and whether the broader clinical picture is being assessed.

The research base for fathers' infant-harm intrusions is still comparatively thin. A UK Health Research Authority summary for a study specifically on new fathers noted that research had focused primarily on mothers and that very few empirical studies had investigated harm intrusions in new fathers. (Health Research Authority, 2020)

A provider should be able to say, in effect, "We know something, we do not know everything, and we can still assess and treat the pattern in front of us."

Action Challenge: Make the First Contact Short

Do not write your whole history into a voicemail.

Use a short request.

"I am a new father having recurrent unwanted intrusive thoughts around my baby. I have started avoiding care and seeking reassurance. I would like an assessment for OCD and related postpartum mental-health concerns. Do you have experience with OCD and ERP?"

If the answer is no, ask whether they can recommend someone who does.

If you are in immediate danger, believe you may act on harmful thoughts, are losing contact with reality, or cannot safely care for the child, do not wait for a routine specialist appointment. Use urgent local services.

Primary Care Can Be a Starting Point

In many systems, the family doctor, general practitioner, primary-care clinician, or another front-line service can help with initial assessment and referral.

Fathers sometimes assume perinatal services are "for the mother" and therefore never mention their own symptoms at baby-related appointments.

The exact route varies by country and health system.

Do not let uncertainty about the perfect door stop you from using an available door.

You can say, "I know this appointment is mainly about the baby, but I am struggling with intrusive thoughts and avoidance and I need to know where fathers can be assessed."

The professional may not be the person who provides OCD treatment.

They may be the person who helps you reach it.

What to Bring to the First Appointment

Bring a one-page pattern summary.

When did it start?

What are the broad themes?

What tasks do you avoid?

What do you check?

What reassurance do you seek?

How much time does it take?

How has it changed parenting or your relationship?

What other symptoms are present?

What medications or substances are relevant?

Are there any safety concerns, intent, planning, or experiences of losing contact with reality?

This page prevents the appointment from becoming a performance in which anxiety decides what you remember.

Do not turn the page into a confession archive.

You need a clinical summary, not a complete catalog of every mental image.

If You Are Afraid of Being Misunderstood

The fear is not irrational in the sense of being impossible.

People can misunderstand mental-health disclosures.

Fathers may also anticipate a different social response to child-harm content because of stereotypes about men, aggression, and caregiving. Evidence on father-specific intrusive-thought disclosure is limited, so we should not pretend we know exactly how often this occurs.

What you can control is the quality of the information you bring.

State that the thoughts are unwanted if that is true.

Describe compulsions and avoidance.

Describe intent or lack of intent accurately rather than strategically.

Mention other symptoms.

Ask how the clinician assesses OCD and risk.

If you feel the provider has misunderstood something, ask them to explain their formulation.

If there is no urgent safety issue and the provider lacks OCD expertise, seeking a specialist opinion may be reasonable.

Accuracy is a better protection than a rehearsed innocence speech.

Medication Is a Clinical Decision

Some fathers want to avoid medication at all costs.

Others want a prescription because they hope it will remove the thoughts.

Both positions can become certainty projects.

Medication decisions depend on diagnosis, symptom severity, medical history, side effects, preferences, other medications, and other clinical factors.

NICE includes SSRIs among treatment options for OCD and gives guidance on how psychological treatment and medication may be considered at different levels of impairment. (National Institute for Health and Care Excellence, 2005)

Talk to a qualified prescriber.

Ask what benefit is realistic.

Ask about side effects.

Ask how long a trial would typically be evaluated.

Ask what to do if symptoms worsen.

Do not stop prescribed medication abruptly without medical advice.

Medication, when used, is not a moral verdict about the seriousness of your fatherhood.

It is a treatment decision.

Telehealth and Geography

A father in a city may have several OCD specialists nearby.

A father in a rural area may have none.

Telehealth can widen access where licensing, jurisdiction, and clinical appropriateness allow it.

Do not assume that an online therapist can legally treat you simply because their website appears in your search results. Check location requirements and credentials.

Directories can help identify clinicians, but a directory listing is not proof of fit.

Ask the same treatment questions.

If cost is a barrier, ask about insurance, public services, training clinics, group treatment, sliding fees where available, or referral options.

There is no shame-free magic route.

There are practical routes, each with tradeoffs.

The Partner Appointment

A partner session can be useful when reassurance and avoidance have redistributed the household.

The purpose is not to decide which partner has the correct emotional reaction.

The purpose is to clarify the cycle.

What reassurance is being requested?

Which tasks are being avoided?

How should a partner respond when the reassurance question appears?

Which fathering tasks are returning and on what schedule?

What symptoms require a different response?

A clinician can help distinguish support from family accommodation.

That distinction protects the partner from becoming an unpaid therapist and protects the father from having treatment depend on the partner saying the right sentence.

Action Challenge: Ask the Accommodation Question

At treatment, ask:

"Which things my partner is doing are genuine support, and which might be helping the OCD cycle continue?"

Then ask the reciprocal question:

"Which responsibilities do I need to resume even while treatment is still in progress?"

Those questions keep recovery connected to family life.

If the First Treatment Does Not Work

A disappointing treatment experience can become a reason to retreat from all care.

Try to be more specific.

Was the diagnosis uncertain?

Was the treatment actually ERP?

Were exposures targeted to your real compulsions?

Were mental rituals addressed?

Did reassurance continue in treatment?

Was the treatment dose sufficient?

Were there other conditions affecting progress?

Could you practice between sessions?

Did practical barriers make attendance irregular?

These are questions for a clinician, not evidence that you are untreatable.

NICE guidance includes stepped approaches and options for more intensive or combined treatment when impairment is greater or earlier approaches have not been enough. (National Institute for Health and Care Excellence, 2005)

A treatment that did not help is data.

It is not a prophecy.

Do Not Build an Expert-Checking Compulsion

Once fathers learn the word ERP, some begin searching for the perfect authority.

They compare credentials.

They read every article.

They ask three clinicians the same diagnostic question.

They search whether the specialist's reassurance can be trusted.

Expertise matters.

But expert shopping can become reassurance when the aim shifts from getting competent care to obtaining an unchallengeable verdict.

Set a reasonable standard.

Does the clinician have appropriate credentials for your location?

Do they have real OCD treatment experience?

Do they use evidence-based methods?

Can they assess the broader clinical picture?

Can you access the treatment consistently?

Then begin the work.

There may always be a more famous expert somewhere.

Your recovery does not need the most famous name.

It needs competent care and sustained practice.

When Depression Is Part of the Picture

OCD can coexist with depression.

Fatherhood itself can also coincide with paternal depression, which has its own evidence base. Meta-analyses have estimated paternal depression across pregnancy and the postpartum period at meaningful rates, although estimates vary by method and time point. (Cameron et al., 2016; Paulson & Bazemore, 2010)

If you have persistent low mood, loss of interest, hopelessness, severe guilt, major changes in functioning, or thoughts of death or suicide, tell the clinician.

Do not assume every symptom is "just the OCD."

If you are in immediate danger of harming yourself, seek emergency help now.

Treating the full clinical picture can make OCD work more feasible.

What Good Help Feels Like

Good treatment may not feel reassuring.

It may feel clear.

You understand what the clinician thinks is happening.

You know what is still uncertain.

You know which behaviors are keeping the loop going.

You know what you are practicing between sessions.

You know what would count as a safety change requiring a different response.

You can ask questions without the session becoming an endless verdict about your character.

That is a more useful standard than whether you leave every appointment calm.

Principles to Remember

Fathers can face practical and cultural barriers to mental-health help, and services do not always feel designed with them in mind. Do not wait to become perfectly certain of the diagnosis before describing the pattern to a qualified professional.

For OCD, know the phrase cognitive behavioral therapy with exposure and response prevention. Ask providers about actual experience with OCD, mental compulsions, reassurance, avoidance, taboo intrusive thoughts, and partner accommodation.

A good assessment considers the whole picture, not just the shocking sentence inside a thought.

Medication decisions belong with a qualified prescriber. Treatment intensity should match impairment and clinical need.

If the first treatment is disappointing, identify what did and did not happen before concluding that nothing will help.

Do not turn specialist shopping into another certainty ritual.

The aim is competent assessment, evidence-based treatment, and a plan that puts you back into ordinary fatherhood.

Chapter 13: The First Two Years Without Retreat

At seventeen months, Owen's son learned to say "mine."

He said it about the red cup, the remote control, a banana he had already abandoned, and the left shoe Owen was trying to put on him.

Nothing about this stage resembled the newborn weeks that had first triggered Owen's intrusive thoughts. The routines were different. The child moved. The hazards changed. Sleep had changed, improved, worsened, and changed again.

The OCD pattern had changed too.

Owen no longer feared nappy changes. That rung had become ordinary months earlier. Now he feared playgrounds. His son climbed too high for Owen's nervous system and not high at all by toddler standards. Owen felt flashes of accidental-harm imagery and the old urge to make his partner handle every risky-looking moment.

For a week he told himself this was a new problem.

Then he recognized the old sequence.

Thought.

Meaning.

Anxiety.

Avoidance.

Relief.

Smaller fatherhood.

The principle of this final chapter is: **the content of the fear can change as your child changes, but you can keep using the same skills to notice retreat early and return to participation.**

The first two years in this book are a practical parenting window, not a claim that all research defines the perinatal period as exactly twenty-four months. The point is that intrusive-thought problems do not necessarily stop because the fourth trimester, first birthday, or another calendar marker has passed.

Fatherhood keeps moving.

Your method has to move with it.

Month Three Is Not Month Eighteen

Newborn care is repetitive and intimate.

Toddler care is mobile and unpredictable.

That changes the places where obsessional doubt can attach itself.

Early fears may center on holding, feeding, nappy changes, bath time, sleep, and being alone with the baby.

Later fears may center on stairs, playgrounds, driving, discipline, frustration, kitchens, illness, accidents, or physical play.

A father who expects recovery to mean "I never get another harm thought" may interpret a new theme as total relapse.

A father who understands the loop can ask a better question:

"What did I start doing because this thought arrived?"

That is often the fastest route back to useful action.

The Early-Retreat Signs

Retreat rarely begins with a dramatic announcement.

It starts with convenience.

"I'll let her do the bath tonight."

"I'll skip the park because I'm tired."

"I'll ask whether she thinks I seem okay."

"I'll check the monitor one more time."

"I'll search this one thing and then stop."

Any one of those behaviors can be ordinary.

The pattern matters.

When the same task gets handed over repeatedly after anxiety spikes, when reassurance questions begin multiplying, or when you add private rules around care, the loop may be rebuilding.

Your early-warning system should watch behavior, not thought frequency alone.

Thoughts can get louder during stress without meaning you have lost all progress.

What matters is whether the old responses are returning with them.

Action Challenge: Write Your Retreat Signature

Finish these five sentences in your own words.

"When I begin retreating, the first task I usually hand over is..."

"The reassurance question I start asking is..."

"The kind of internet search I start doing is..."

"The body or memory check I start doing is..."

"The ordinary part of fatherhood that gets smaller first is..."

Keep the answers somewhere you can find them.

The point is not self-surveillance.

It is earlier recognition.

Stress Makes Old Roads Easy to Find

OCD spikes do not happen in a vacuum.

A child's illness.

A job deadline.

Relationship conflict.

Another pregnancy.

Moving house.

Bereavement.

Sleep disruption.

Financial pressure.

Any of these can leave you with less attention and patience.

The old compulsion is familiar. Familiar behaviors are easier to fall into under strain.

That does not mean stress "causes" every OCD spike in a simple way.

It means your maintenance plan should include the reality that family life will not remain calm long enough for you to finish recovery.

You need a plan that works during ordinary difficulty.

The Bad Week Rule

Marcus used one simple maintenance rule.

A bad week could change the size of a task.

It could not silently erase the task from his role.

If he was exhausted, the solo outing might shrink from two hours to thirty minutes.

If the child was ill, normal caregiving needs took priority over exposure planning.

If his anxiety spiked, he contacted his therapist.

What he tried not to do was say, "Let's pause all of my feared parenting tasks until I feel like myself again."

That sentence had cost him months before.

Flexibility is not retreat.

Retreat is when anxiety becomes the permanent scheduler.

Sleep Deserves Respect Without Becoming an OCD Explanation

Parents lose sleep.

Sleep affects mood, attention, irritability, and coping.

Severe sleep disruption can also complicate mental-health symptoms.

Do not treat sleep as irrelevant.

Do not treat every bad night as proof that you are unsafe either.

If sleep loss is severe, persistent, or accompanied by concerning changes in mood, behavior, judgment, reality testing, or functioning, tell a healthcare professional.

For ordinary exhaustion, build practical support where possible.

Trade shifts.

Use available family help.

Protect sleep opportunities.

The key is to distinguish support for a tired parent from a rule that says, "I am forbidden to care for my child unless I feel perfectly rested."

Perfectly rested may not be a category available to you this year.

When Anger Returns

Toddlers can bring a new kind of frustration.

They refuse.

They repeat.

They do the dangerous thing immediately after you explain the dangerous thing.

A father who has spent months treating any irritation as evidence may discover that toddlerhood gives him more evidence than he knows what to do with.

Return to the distinction from Chapter 6.

Anger is a state.

Behavior matters.

If you are concerned about aggressive behavior, losing control, substance use, or safety, get direct assessment and use an appropriate safety plan.

If the fear is obsessional and the behavior is not unsafe, do not conduct a moral inquiry every time your jaw tightens.

Learn ordinary regulation.

Learn ordinary parenting strategies.

Take appropriate breaks.

Repair when you are sharp.

Do not demand that love remove irritation from human parenting.

Repair Is a Parenting Skill

You will get things wrong that have nothing to do with OCD.

You will use the wrong tone.

You will forget the cup.

You will miss the sign that the child is overtired.

You will argue with your partner.

You may become impatient.

A father caught in perfectionistic responsibility can turn normal mistakes into a week-long moral audit.

That audit is not repair.

Repair is concrete.

"I was too sharp with you. I'm sorry."

"I said I would do bedtime and I handed it back because I was anxious. I want to take it tonight."

"I missed the appointment. I have rescheduled it."

You do not need to resolve your entire character before correcting a behavior.

That is a useful principle far beyond OCD.

The Partner's Memory May Be Different From Yours

Your partner may remember the first months as a period when they carried far too much.

You may remember them as the period when you were terrified.

Both memories can be true.

Recovery can tempt a family to avoid the old story entirely. Nobody wants to reopen it.

Sometimes a brief, structured conversation helps.

"What did my avoidance cost you?"

"What are you still worried will happen if symptoms return?"

"What do you need from me that is practical rather than reassuring?"

"What should we do if I begin handing tasks back?"

Do not demand immediate forgiveness.

Do not use guilt as a reason to overcompensate with unsustainable promises.

Build reliability in the present.

Action Challenge: Make the Relapse Agreement

With your partner, if appropriate, agree on three signs that the OCD loop is taking over family routines again.

Then agree on three actions.

One treatment action: contact the clinician or return to the plan.

One household action: preserve or restore a specific fathering responsibility where safe and appropriate.

One communication action: name reassurance without turning the partner into the judge.

Keep the agreement short.

A plan you can remember during a bad week is more useful than a beautiful document nobody opens.

The Child Does Not Need Your Internal Report

One of the strangest freedoms in recovery is realizing that your child does not require access to the meeting happening in your head.

Your toddler can sit on your lap while your mind produces nonsense.

You can make breakfast while anxiety is high.

You can sing badly while your brain runs a threat simulation.

You can be present before you feel resolved.

This matters because OCD makes fatherhood feel conditional.

When I know what the thought means, then I can relax into being a dad.

The order can be reversed.

You can do the dad part while the mind remains noisy.

That is values-led parenting.

What to Tell Yourself About a New Theme

Be careful here.

A coping phrase can become reassurance if you repeat it to force anxiety down.

The aim is not to find a sentence that neutralizes the thought.

The aim is to orient yourself toward process.

"This is a new theme, but I recognize the checking urge."

"I don't need to decide what this thought means before I finish breakfast."

"I will bring the pattern to treatment instead of solving it in the bathroom."

"I can use reasonable safety without demanding certainty."

These statements point toward behavior.

They do not certify character.

When a Second Child Arrives

Another pregnancy or baby can reactivate old fears.

You may feel embarrassed.

"I already dealt with this."

But a new child creates new sleep patterns, new responsibilities, new triggers, and new uncertainty.

Use what you learned early.

Tell your clinician sooner.

Tell your partner sooner.

Watch for the first avoidance.

Keep the Stay-In Ladder ready.

Do not wait until the feared task has been absent from your life for three months.

Prior recovery is not a guarantee against recurrence.

It is prior training.

When Treatment Ends

Treatment ending can trigger one last certainty demand.

"How will I know I am really done?"

You may want a final percentage.

A final assurance.

A final promise that the thoughts will not return.

A more realistic end point is behavioral.

You know what the OCD cycle looks like for you.

You can identify your common compulsions.

You participate in ordinary fathering tasks.

You can tolerate intrusive thoughts without automatically neutralizing them.

You know when to seek help.

You have a plan for setbacks.

That is enough to graduate from constant symptom management into ordinary life, even though ordinary life still contains uncertainty.

The First Birthday Problem

Milestones can become scorecards.

The first birthday arrives and you think about everything you missed.

The baths.

The solo walks.

The weeks you refused nappies.

The photos where you stood at the edge.

Regret can be useful when it points to a changed behavior.

It becomes corrosive when it demands that you recover the past before you are allowed to enjoy the present.

You cannot do the missed bath from seven months ago.

You can do tonight's.

You cannot become the father you wish you had been in month two.

You can choose what you do in month thirteen.

This book is about that choice.

The Second Birthday Question

By the second birthday, the child may have no memory of the earliest crisis in the way you do.

You may still carry it vividly.

Ask a practical question:

"What is OCD still deciding in our family?"

Maybe the answer is nothing major.

Good.

Maybe you still avoid the playground.

Maybe your partner still does every bath.

Maybe you still ask for reassurance after discipline.

Maybe a taboo theme remains secret from treatment.

Choose one place where the loop still owns a rule.

That is the next piece of work.

Recovery does not have to be dramatic to continue.

Action Challenge: The Two-Year Inventory

Review the domains this book has covered.

Solo care.

Nappies and bathing.

Stairs and kitchens.

Driving.

Play.

Bedtime.

Anger and shutdown.

Partner communication.

Reassurance.

Mental review.

Body checking.

Help-seeking.

For each domain, write one of three words: "ordinary," "shrunk," or "unclear."

Ordinary means the task is part of family life without major OCD rules.

Shrunk means fear has reduced your participation.

Unclear means you cannot tell whether the current pattern is reasonable safety, practical family choice, or avoidance.

Take the shrunk items to your Stay-In Ladder.

Take the unclear items to a clinician or other relevant professional.

Do not build a new twelve-page audit.

One page is enough.

Your Child Will Keep Changing

There is no final version of fatherhood.

The baby becomes a toddler.

The toddler becomes a child who asks questions.

New fears can appear around school, illness, independence, discipline, sexuality, driving, and a hundred other things.

This book stops at two years because a book needs edges.

The larger skill does not stop.

Notice the thought.

Notice the meaning you attach to it.

Notice the compulsion.

Choose reasonable safety.

Return to the value.

Stay in the relationship.

Get help when the picture changes.

The method is portable.

Keep One Small Piece of Ordinary Life Nonclinical

There is value in having part of fatherhood that you do not score.

A Saturday pancake.

A ridiculous song.

A walk to the same corner shop.

A five-minute game with blocks.

Do not rate anxiety afterward. Do not turn it into an exposure log. Let it be part of family life.

Treatment is supposed to return you to living. It is not supposed to become the permanent manager of every interaction with your child. As your skills strengthen, more of fatherhood should move back into the category of ordinary.

That is one reason the book ends here.

Not because the work can never continue, but because the work should eventually make more room for everything else.

Principles to Remember

Recovery is not proved by never having another intrusive thought. The content can change as your child changes.

Watch behavior for early signs of retreat: handed-over tasks, repeated reassurance, checking, new private rules, and shrinking participation.

Stress can make old compulsions easier to reach. Build a maintenance plan that assumes family life will sometimes be hard.

Normal parenting mistakes require repair, not a moral trial.

Your partner's account of the difficult months may differ from yours. Let treatment explain the pattern without using it to erase impact.

A second child, a new theme, or a bad week can reactivate old fear. Prior recovery is not a warranty. It is training.

The first two years are not a deadline for being finished.

They are a large enough stretch of fatherhood to prove something more useful: you can keep returning, steadily, even when certainty never arrives on schedule.

Conclusion: The Dad Who Stayed

The father in the title of this book is not a special kind of man.

He is not fearless.

He is not perfectly calm.

He is not the father who found the one argument strong enough to defeat every intrusive thought.

He is the father who learned what the thought was doing to his behavior and stopped letting it decide every piece of care.

At the beginning, the problem may have looked like one horrifying mental event.

A thought during bath time.

An image on the stairs.

A taboo idea during a nappy change.

A sudden question about what you might be capable of.

Then the thought acquired a system.

Avoid the task.

Ask your partner.

Check your body.

Review your memory.

Search.

Confess.

Wait to feel certain.

Fatherhood became smaller while the case against you became larger.

That is the part nobody warns many fathers about. The thought can be brief. The response can take over months.

What You Know Now

You know that intrusive thoughts are mental events, not automatic verdicts.

You know that content alone does not diagnose OCD and does not settle risk.

You know why assessment matters.

You know how harm obsessions can recruit thought-action fusion, inflated responsibility, reassurance, mental review, body checking, avoidance, confession, and family accommodation.

You know why a partner can support you without becoming the person who repeatedly certifies your safety.

You know why anger deserves its own careful look rather than being used as either proof of danger or a supposedly "male" OCD symptom.

You know the difference between ordinary childcare safety and the certainty trap.

You know the phrase CBT with exposure and response prevention.

And you know how to use the Stay-In Ladder to translate a global fear into a specific piece of fatherhood you can work toward.

None of that gives you a guarantee.

It gives you a method.

The Method in One Page

When the intrusive thought arrives, notice the next move.

What meaning are you assigning to the thought?

What are you about to do to obtain certainty?

Are you avoiding?

Checking?

Reviewing?

Reassurance-seeking?

Confessing?

Monitoring your body?

Handing the task over?

Then separate two questions.

Is there an actual safety concern that needs assessment or ordinary parenting action?

Or is the mind demanding a level of certainty that no parent can obtain?

If safety is genuinely uncertain, get appropriate in-person help.

If the pattern is obsessional and the caregiving action is appropriate, choose the next values-led step.

Do the task.

Reduce the compulsion you and your clinician have identified.

Let uncertainty remain unfinished.

Return to the child.

That is the method.

The Work Is Behavioral Before It Is Inspirational

Books like this can end with a speech about courage.

Courage is useful.

A schedule is often more useful.

What bath are you doing this week?

Which solo-care block is yours?

What reassurance question are you going to stop asking your partner?

Which appointment are you making?

What task belongs on the next rung of your Stay-In Ladder?

What will you do after the task instead of conducting a postmortem?

Recovery becomes visible in ordinary calendar entries.

Tuesday bath.

Thursday nursery pickup.

Saturday breakfast.

Twenty minutes at the playground.

One appointment you actually attend.

These actions are not small because they look small.

They are the substance of fatherhood.

If You Still Feel Unsure

You may reach the final pages and still have the question that brought you here.

"What if my thoughts mean something terrible?"

A book cannot answer that question for a particular person.

That is not a failure of the book.

It is a boundary that protects you from using the book as reassurance.

If you have not been assessed and the pattern is impairing your life, seek an OCD-informed evaluation.

If you have intent, planning, a wish to act, loss of contact with reality, or any reason immediate safety is uncertain, seek urgent in-person help.

If you have been assessed and you recognize the reassurance loop, notice what you are asking the final page to do.

You may be asking it to give you one last certificate.

It cannot.

It can remind you what to practice next.

The Partner Who Has Carried Too Much

If your avoidance has left your partner with more childcare, recovery includes more than reducing your anxiety.

It includes contribution.

That may mean returning to tasks gradually while taking on other household work immediately.

It may mean hearing your partner's anger without turning the conversation into a defense of your diagnosis.

It may mean saying, "This explains why I disappeared from that part of parenting. It does not make the cost disappear."

A mental-health explanation is not a moral acquittal or conviction.

It is information.

Use the information to change what happens next.

The Child in Front of You

OCD pulls attention away from the child and toward the father as a problem to be solved.

What did I think?

What did I feel?

What does it mean?

What if?

The child keeps doing what children do while the internal hearing continues.

They need a bottle.

They throw the spoon.

They laugh at something that is not funny.

They refuse the coat.

They demand the same story.

They wake too early.

They become a toddler.

The most radical move in this entire book is often the least dramatic one.

Return attention to the child in front of you.

Not because attention makes the thought disappear.

Because this is the relationship you were trying to protect.

A Final Stay-In Step

Choose one task you have been postponing because you wanted to feel more certain first.

Make it appropriately small.

Make it behaviorally clear.

Make sure it does not conflict with real safety requirements or professional advice.

Name the compulsion you expect.

Name the after-plan.

Then schedule the step.

Do not schedule a feeling.

Do not write, "When I feel ready."

Write a day.

If you are in treatment, bring the step to your clinician.

If you need an assessment first, make that the step.

The Stay-In Ladder always begins where you actually are.

What Staying Means

Staying does not mean never leaving a room.

It does not mean ignoring exhaustion.

It does not mean refusing help.

It does not mean forcing yourself through symptoms that require urgent assessment.

It means refusing to let obsessional doubt quietly become the architect of your relationship with your child.

It means coming back after avoidance.

It means participating while your mind is noisy.

It means allowing reasonable safety to be reasonable rather than absolute.

It means asking for skilled help without requiring the clinician to give you permanent certainty.

It means letting fatherhood contain more than fear.

You may still have intrusive thoughts.

You may still have bad weeks.

You may still need treatment.

You can also change a nappy, run a bath, read the book, carry the bag, take the shift, go to the appointment, cook the dinner, push the swing, and stay for the ordinary part.

That is not a lesser victory because nobody sees it.

It is the point.

The father nobody warned can become the father who knows what to do next.

Not because the mind finally became silent.

Because he stopped waiting for silence before he showed up.

Resources: A 30-Day Stay-In Plan

This section is a practice guide, not a treatment protocol and not a substitute for assessment. If you have intent, planning, a wish to act, loss of contact with reality, severe impairment, intoxication, or any reason you are uncertain that you or your child is safe, use appropriate urgent in-person services rather than a self-guided exercise.

If your presentation has been assessed as OCD or is being evaluated as an obsessional pattern, use these thirty days as a way to organize participation, notice compulsions, and prepare useful material for treatment.

The plan is deliberately simple. Do not improve it into a complicated tracking system.

Days 1 to 3: Observe the Loop

For three days, do not try to fix everything.

Notice one intrusive thought episode per day and record four facts in a sentence or two: the situation, the meaning your mind assigned to the thought, the compulsion or avoidance urge that followed, and what the episode cost in time or participation.

An entry might read:

"During bedtime I had a harm image, interpreted it as evidence I could lose control, asked my partner twice if I seemed okay, and handed the last part of bedtime back to her."

Another might read:

"During a nappy change I had a taboo thought, checked my body and memory afterward, and spent twenty minutes reviewing the task."

Do not catalog every thought.

You are looking for structure.

At the end of day three, circle the response that appears most often: reassurance, checking, mental review, body monitoring, confession, internet searching, avoidance, or another neutralizing behavior.

That is your first working target.

Days 4 to 5: Separate Safety From Certainty

Choose two feared situations.

For each, write what ordinary parenting safety requires.

Then write what OCD appears to demand in addition.

For example:

Ordinary safety may require fitting a car seat correctly.

OCD may demand photographing the buckle, reopening it three times, and asking your partner to inspect it.

Ordinary bath safety requires appropriate supervision.

OCD may demand that another adult remain in the doorway because your mind produced an unwanted thought.

If you cannot tell which precautions are ordinary and which are obsessional, do not guess. Bring the question to a qualified clinician or an appropriate childcare professional.

The purpose of these two days is not to remove safeguards.

It is to make the certainty trap visible.

Days 6 to 7: Write the Help-Seeking Script

If you are not already in appropriate care and the pattern is impairing fatherhood, write your first-contact message.

Keep it short.

"I am a father experiencing recurrent unwanted intrusive thoughts around my child. I have started avoiding care and using reassurance and checking. I would like an assessment for OCD and related mental-health concerns. Do you have experience with CBT that includes exposure and response prevention?"

Add any urgent or important symptoms honestly.

Make the contact.

If the first provider is not a fit, ask for a referral.

Do not spend the whole week comparing experts online before contacting anyone.

Days 8 to 9: Map the Missing Fatherhood

List five pieces of fatherhood that have become smaller since the intrusive-thought loop began.

Be concrete.

"Tuesday bath."

"Solo walk to the park."

"Morning nappy changes."

"Cooking while the baby is nearby."

"Bedtime when my partner goes out."

Now rank them by family value, not just fear.

Which missing task matters most to your relationship with your child or to the fairness of the household?

That task is a candidate for your Stay-In Ladder.

Days 10 to 11: Build Four Rungs

Take one valued task and create four observable re-entry steps.

Do not write emotional goals such as "feel safe."

Write behaviors.

If your goal is solo bedtime, a lower rung might be doing the whole routine while your partner is elsewhere in the home. A later rung might be doing it while your partner is out, if that is clinically appropriate and consistent with ordinary childcare needs.

Next to each rung, write the compulsion you expect.

"Reassurance after the task."

"Keeping the door open as a safety signal."

"Body checking."

"Reviewing the whole routine in bed."

If you are in ERP treatment, review the ladder with your clinician.

Day 12: Plan the After-Plan

Choose what you will do immediately after the rung.

Keep it ordinary.

Put away the towel.

Make tea.

Prepare the bottle for tomorrow.

Read something.

Talk to your partner about the day.

Your after-plan exists because mental review often arrives late.

Write one sentence naming what you will practice not doing after the task.

"After bath time, I will not replay how I held my child."

Do not turn the after-plan into a distraction ritual whose purpose is to make anxiety vanish.

Its purpose is to help you return to ordinary life without opening the mental courtroom.

Days 13 to 15: Practice One Rung Three Times

Repeat the first meaningful rung three times if that schedule is appropriate.

Track only three things.

Did I participate?

Which compulsion did I reduce?

What would I adjust next time?

You may note an anxiety rating if your clinician uses one, but do not make low anxiety the definition of success.

A practice can be useful while anxiety is high.

A practice can be unhelpful while anxiety is low if you spent the entire time neutralizing.

At the end of the third attempt, decide with your clinician or plan whether to repeat, adjust, or move up.

Day 16: Audit Reassurance

For one day, notice every time you ask someone else to settle a question about what your thought means.

Do not count ordinary requests for information.

"Did the pediatrician say the appointment is at two?" is information.

"Do you think I looked dangerous when I was holding him?" may be reassurance.

"Can you show me how this buckle works?" may be information.

"Can you check it a fifth time so I can feel sure?" may be reassurance.

Function matters.

At the end of the day, choose one repeated reassurance question to work on.

Day 17: Give Your Partner a Different Role

If you have a partner and it is appropriate, explain the reassurance question you are trying to reduce.

Agree on a response that does not become a debate.

Your partner might say, "I think that is the OCD question. What does your treatment plan say?"

Or, "I can support you while you continue the task, but I am not going to answer the certainty question."

The exact wording matters less than consistency.

Your partner is not required to become your therapist.

If the household has been carrying the cost of your avoidance, also choose one practical contribution you can make reliably.

Day 18: Separate the Symptom Conversation From the Workload Conversation

Have two short conversations instead of one long argument.

In the symptom conversation, discuss the OCD plan, treatment, reassurance, and accommodation.

In the workload conversation, discuss who is doing baths, nappies, cooking, night care, appointments, and other responsibilities.

A mental-health explanation can make behavior understandable.

It does not automatically make the workload fair.

Choose one task distribution change that can happen now.

Day 19: Find the Invisible Job

During one routine care task, notice the ordinary job and the invisible OCD job.

Ordinary job: feed the baby.

Invisible job: prove I had no bad thought while doing it.

Ordinary job: hold my toddler's hand on the stairs.

Invisible job: guarantee I could never make a mistake.

Ordinary job: change the nappy.

Invisible job: monitor every body sensation.

Return attention to the ordinary job.

Let the invisible job remain unfinished.

Day 20: Drop One Safety Signal

Choose one safety signal that your clinician agrees is unnecessary.

It may be requiring your partner to stay in the room.

It may be recording yourself.

It may be texting repeatedly during solo care.

It may be moving an ordinary object only because the thought appeared.

Drop or reduce one signal during a planned task.

Do not remove ordinary child-safety practices.

The exercise is not "be less safe."

It is "stop using extra rituals to manufacture certainty."

Day 21: Practice a Normal Reset

Parents need breaks.

Plan what an ordinary reset looks like for you.

Perhaps the baby is placed safely in the cot while you take a brief moment to regulate.

Perhaps you and your partner trade places because that is the agreed household rhythm.

Perhaps you drink water and return.

Now write what turns a reset into retreat.

"I cancel the rest of my shift because an intrusive thought appeared."

"I refuse to resume the task until I feel certain."

"I call my partner home every time anxiety spikes."

The goal is flexible regulation without making every spike a reason to disappear.

Days 22 to 23: Reclaim Play

Choose one piece of physical or ordinary play that fear has shrunk.

Five minutes on the floor.

Pushing the swing.

Building blocks.

Reading with your child on your lap.

Walking to the park.

Keep the task age-appropriate and ordinarily safe.

Do not grade the quality of your feelings.

Notice whether self-monitoring tries to pull attention inward.

Return to the activity.

Children are excellent at producing unscripted details. Let some of those details back into the scene.

Day 24: Check the Expert-Checking Loop

Search history can reveal a hidden compulsion.

Look at the mental-health searches you have made in the last week.

Were they for practical access to care?

Or were you repeatedly searching different versions of the same moral question?

Delete saved tabs that function mainly as reassurance if doing so fits your treatment plan.

Choose one reliable source for practical information and one treatment contact.

Then stop collecting opinions for the day.

Competent care matters.

An infinite jury does not.

Day 25: Review Other Symptoms

Do not force the whole picture into OCD.

Write down whether you have noticed persistent low mood, major loss of interest, severe guilt, substance use, unusual energy or agitation, significant changes in sleep beyond childcare demands, experiences of losing contact with reality, or thoughts of harming yourself.

This is not a diagnostic checklist.

It is a prompt to give your clinician the complete picture.

If there is immediate risk, use urgent services.

If there are important nonurgent symptoms, bring them to your next appointment.

Treating the right problem requires seeing more than the most frightening thought.

Day 26: Repair One Concrete Cost

Choose one thing your avoidance has cost the household.

Do not write an apology essay.

Repair behaviorally.

Resume a task.

Make the appointment you postponed.

Take a predictable shift.

Acknowledge the impact without demanding reassurance that your partner understands.

A useful sentence is:

"I know the OCD pattern contributed to this, and I also know it left more work with you. Here is the piece I am taking back."

Then follow through.

Day 27: Move One Rung

If the earlier practice has been appropriate and repeatable, move one step higher on your Stay-In Ladder.

Keep response prevention attached.

Do not celebrate progression by adding a new ritual.

If the rung feels dramatically beyond your plan, adjust with your clinician rather than making the day a bravery contest.

The ladder is supposed to build learning and participation, not produce a story about how much fear you can endure.

Day 28: Write the Bad-Week Rule

Finish this sentence:

"When I have a bad week, I may make the task smaller, but I will not silently erase __________ from my fathering role."

Then write the person you will contact if avoidance starts expanding again.

Choose an early threshold.

For example:

"If I hand over the same feared task three times in one week because of intrusive thoughts, I will contact my therapist."

The exact threshold is yours.

The point is to decide before the retreat feels reasonable.

Day 29: Make the Relapse Agreement

If you have a partner, agree on three observable signs that the loop is rebuilding.

Examples include repeated reassurance, handing over a specific task, reopening a body-checking ritual, or increasing internet searches.

Then agree on three responses.

A treatment response.

A household response.

A communication response.

Keep it short.

Do not make your partner responsible for policing every thought.

The agreement is about behavior both of you can see.

Day 30: Choose the Next Month of Fatherhood

Do not finish by scoring the month.

Choose the next valued behavior.

Maybe you keep the current rung and make it reliable.

Maybe you move up.

Maybe you begin a second ladder for a different task.

Maybe the most important action is finally attending the specialist appointment.

Write one line:

"Next month, the piece of fatherhood I am building is ___________."

Then put it on the calendar.

The purpose of these thirty days is not to make intrusive thoughts disappear.

It is to make your response to them more visible, more deliberate, and less able to shrink your role without your consent.

A Short Provider Checklist

When you contact a clinician, you can keep these questions nearby.

Ask whether they assess and treat OCD.

Ask whether they use CBT that includes exposure and response prevention.

Ask how they work with mental compulsions, reassurance, avoidance, and family accommodation.

Ask how they approach taboo intrusive thoughts and risk assessment.

Ask how partner involvement is handled.

Ask what to do if symptoms change in a way that raises a new safety concern.

You do not need a provider who promises certainty.

You need a provider who can assess carefully and treat the cycle competently.

A Short Partner Checklist

If you are the partner reading this section, your role is not to decide what every thought means.

You can encourage assessment.

You can learn the difference between support and repeated reassurance.

You can help identify avoidance that has changed family routines.

You can set boundaries around graphic detail or repetitive checking conversations.

You can ask for household responsibilities to be rebuilt.

You can seek your own support if the situation has exhausted or frightened you.

If there is a genuine safety concern, use professional help rather than trying to manage it alone at home.

A Short Urgent-Help Boundary

This book is designed for education and behavior change around intrusive-thought and OCD patterns.

It is not an emergency service.

Seek urgent local in-person help when there is intent or planning to harm, a wish to act, inability to keep someone safe, loss of contact with reality, severe agitation or confusion, or another acute change that makes immediate safety uncertain.

If you are in the United States and are in suicidal or mental-health crisis, you can call or text 988 or use the 988 Lifeline chat. In other countries, use your local emergency number or national crisis service. (988 Lifeline, n.d.)

If you are not in immediate danger but the symptoms are impairing parenting, work, sleep, or relationships, arrange a qualified mental-health assessment rather than waiting for the pattern to become unmistakable.

The best time to get help is not when you have finally solved the thought.

It is when you can describe what the loop is costing you.

About the Author

Mason R. Ellery writes practical nonfiction about the parts of family life that are often difficult to name. His work emphasizes precise language, evidence-informed explanation, and concrete actions readers can use without pretending uncertainty can be eliminated. He writes for people who want a calm guide through complicated subjects, with respect for clinical boundaries and for the difference between education and individualized care.

References

988 Lifeline. (n.d.). Get help. https://988lifeline.org/get-help/

Abramowitz, J. S., Khandker, M., Nelson, C. A., Deacon, B. J., & Rygwall, R. (2006). The role of cognitive factors in the pathogenesis of obsessive-compulsive symptoms: A prospective study. Behaviour Research and Therapy, 44(9), 1361-1374. https://doi.org/10.1016/j.brat.2005.09.011

Abramowitz, J. S., Moore, K., Carmin, C., Wiegartz, P. S., & Purdon, C. (2001). Acute onset of obsessive-compulsive disorder in males following childbirth. Psychosomatics, 42(5), 429-431. https://doi.org/10.1176/appi.psy.42.5.429

Abramowitz, J. S., Nelson, C. A., Rygwall, R., & Khandker, M. (2007). The cognitive mediation of obsessive-compulsive symptoms: A longitudinal study. Journal of Anxiety Disorders, 21(1), 91-104. https://doi.org/10.1016/j.janxdis.2006.05.003

Cameron, E. E., Sedov, I. D., & Tomfohr-Madsen, L. M. (2016). Prevalence of paternal depression in pregnancy and the postpartum: An updated meta-analysis. Journal of Affective Disorders, 206, 189-203. https://doi.org/10.1016/j.jad.2016.07.044

Health Research Authority. (2020). Intrusive thoughts of harm in new fathers. https://www.hra.nhs.uk/planning-and-improving-research/application-summaries/research-summaries/intrusive-thoughts-of-harm-in-new-fathers/

Hudak, R., & Wisner, K. L. (2012). Diagnosis and treatment of postpartum obsessions and compulsions that involve infant harm. American Journal of Psychiatry, 169(4), 360-363. https://doi.org/10.1176/appi.ajp.2011.11050667

International OCD Foundation. (n.d.). What is perinatal OCD? https://iocdf.org/perinatal-ocd/what-is-perinatal-ocd/

National Institute for Health and Care Excellence. (2005). Obsessive-compulsive disorder and body dysmorphic disorder: Treatment (CG31). https://www.nice.org.uk/guidance/cg31/chapter/Recommendations

Paulson, J. F., & Bazemore, S. D. (2010). Prenatal and postpartum depression in fathers and its association with maternal depression: A meta-analysis. JAMA, 303(19), 1961-1969. https://doi.org/10.1001/jama.2010.605

Pedersen, S. C., Maindal, H. T., & Ryom, K. (2021). "I wanted to be there as a father, but I couldn't": A qualitative study of fathers' experiences of postpartum depression and their help-seeking behavior. American Journal of Men's Health, 15(3), 15579883211024375. https://doi.org/10.1177/15579883211024375

Reay, M., Mayers, A., Knowles-Bevis, R., & Knight, M. T. D. (2024). Understanding the barriers fathers face to seeking help for paternal perinatal depression: Comparing fathers to men outside the perinatal period. International Journal of Environmental Research and Public Health, 21(1), 16. https://doi.org/10.3390/ijerph21010016

Shafran, R., & Rachman, S. (2004). Thought-action fusion: A review. Journal of Behavior Therapy and Experimental Psychiatry, 35(2), 87-107. https://doi.org/10.1016/j.jbtep.2004.04.002

www.ingramcontent.com/pod-product-compliance
Lightning Source LLC
LaVergne TN
LVHW010721061126
851857LV00014B/1287
9781911838746